CliffsNotes

Writing Your First Computer Program

By Allen Wyatt

IN THIS BOOK

- Explore the steps and pitfalls of computer programming
- Find out about debugging tools and useful shortcuts
- Use QBasic to write and run your first program
- Reinforce what you learn with CliffsNotes Review
- Find more information about computer programming in the CliffsNotes Resource Center and online at www.cliffsnotes.com

IDG Books Worldwide, Inc.
An International Data Group Company
Foster City, CA • Chicago, IL • Indianapolis, IN • New York, NY

About the Author

Allen Wyatt, an internationally recognized expert in small computer systems, has written more than 35 books explaining many different facets of working with computers, as well as numerous magazine articles. His books have covered topics ranging from computer languages to using application software to using operating systems.

Publisher's Acknowledgments

Editorial

Project Editor: Paul Levesque

Acquisitions Editor: Greg Croy

Copy Editor: Stephanie Koutek

Technical Editor: Namir Shammas

Production

Indexer: York Production Services, Inc.

Proofreader: York Production Services, Inc.

IDG Books Indianapolis Production Department

CliffsNotes™ Writing Your First Computer Program

Published by

IDG Books Worldwide, Inc.

An International Data Group Company

919 E. Hillsdale Blvd. Suite 400

Foster City, CA 94404

www.idgbooks.com (IDG Books Worldwide Web Site)

www.cliffsnotes.com (CliffsNotes Web Site)

Library of Congress Catalog Card No.: 99-66718

ISBN: 0-7645-8523-1

Printed in the United States of America

10 9 8 7 6 5 4 3 2 1

10/SZ/RR/ZZ/IN

Distributed in the United States by IDG Books Worldwide, Inc.

Distributed by CDG Books Canada Inc. for Canada; by Transworld Publishers Limited in the United Kingdom; by IDG Norge Books for Norway; by IDG Sweden Books for Sweden; by IDG Books Australia Publishing Corporation Pty. Ltd. for Australia and New Zealand; by TransQuest Publishers Pte Ltd. for Singapore, Malaysia, Thailand, Indonesia, and Hong Kong; by Gotop Information Inc. for Taiwan; by ICG Muse, Inc. for Japan; by Norma Comunicaciones S.A. for Colombia; by Intersoft for South Africa; by Eyrolles for France; by International Thomson Publishing for Germany, Austria and Switzerland; by Distribuidora Cuspide for Argentina; by LR International for Brazil; by Galileo Libros for Chile; by Ediciones ZETA S.C.R. Ltda. for Peru; by WS Computer Publishing Corporation, Inc., for the Philippines; by Contemporanea de Ediciones for Venezuela; by Express Computer Distributors for the Caribbean and West Indies; by Micronesia Media Distributor, Inc. for Micronesia; by Grupo Editorial Norma S.A. for Guatemala; by Chips Computadoras S.A. de C.V. for Mexico; by Editorial Norma de Panama S.A. for Panama; by American Bookshops for Finland. Authorized Sales Agent: Anthony Rudkin Associates for the Middle East and North Africa.

For general information on IDG Books Worldwide's books in the U.S., please call our Consumer Customer Service department at 800-762-2974. For reseller information, including discounts and premium sales, please call our Reseller Customer Service department at 800-434-3422.

For information on where to purchase IDG Books Worldwide's books outside the U.S., please contact our International Sales department at 317-596-5530 or fax 317-596-5692.

For consumer information on foreign language translations, please contact our Customer Service department at 1-800-434-3422, fax 317-596-5692, or e-mail rights@idgbooks.com.

For information on licensing foreign or domestic rights, please phone +1-650-655-3109.

For sales inquiries and special prices for bulk quantities, please contact our Sales department at 650-655-3200 or write to the address above.

For information on using IDG Books Worldwide's books in the classroom or for ordering examination copies, please contact our Educational Sales department at 800-434-2086 or fax 317-596-5499.

For press review copies, author interviews, or other publicity information, please contact our Public Relations department at 650-655-3000 or fax 650-655-3299.

For authorization to photocopy items for corporate, personal, or educational use, please contact Copyright Clearance Center, 222 Rosewood Drive, Danvers, MA 01923, or fax 978-750-4470.

is a registered trademark under exclusive license to IDG Books Worldwide, Inc., from International Data Group, Inc.

Table of Contents

INTRODUCTION

Computers are all around us. We use them and they, in turn, touch every part of our lives. Everything from thermostats to televisions and dishwashers to car washes is loaded with computers.

These ubiquitous devices don't do their work by magic — although it may seem that way at times. Instead, computers need to be programmed so they know what to do. Programmers carefully script each task and operation well before the computer is put to work.

Programming is not a black art. It is challenging, fun, and at times frustrating. Virtually anyone can be a programmer — even you!

Why Do You Need This Book?

Can you answer yes to any of these questions?

- Do you want to quickly learn the basics of programming?
- Are you looking for a challenging way to expand your knowledge?
- Are you tired of wading through books that should be sold by the pound?

If so, CliffsNotes *Writing Your First Computer Program* is for you!

How to Use This Book

You can read this book straight through or just look for the information you need. You can find information on a particular topic in a number of ways. You can search the index in the back of the book, locate your topic in the Table of

Contents, or read the In This Chapter list in each chapter. To reinforce your learning, check out the Review and Resource Center at the back of the book. Also, to find important information quickly, you can look for icons strategically placed in the text. Here is a description of the icons you'll find in this book:

This icon points out something worth keeping in mind.

This icon clues you in to helpful hints and advice.

This icon alerts you to something dangerous or to avoid.

Don't Miss Our Web Site

Keep up with the exciting world of computer programming by visiting the CliffsNotes Web site at www.cliffs-notes.com. Here's what you'll find:

- Interactive tools that are fun and informative
- Links to interesting Web sites
- Additional resources to help you continue your learning

At www.cliffsnotes.com, you can even register for Cliffs Notes Daily, a free daily newsletter on a variety of topics that we deliver right to your e-mail inbox each business day.

If you haven't yet discovered the Internet and are wondering how to get online, pick up CliffsNotes *Getting On the Internet*, new from CliffsNotes. You'll learn just what you need to make your online connection quickly and easily. See you at www.cliffsnotes.com!

CHAPTER 1

PROGRAMMING LANGUAGE OVERVIEW

IN THIS CHAPTER

- ■ Why programming languages are necessary
- ■ What types of languages are available
- ■ How to pick a programming language
- ■ The importance of syntax

Welcome to the wild and wooly world of computer programming! You may be a bit hesitant to enter this world; you may not even be sure why you have to. Rest assured that even though computer programming looks foreboding right now, learning the basics of using programming languages is not terribly difficult.

Why Use Languages?

Take a close look at your computer. What do you see? A monitor that looks like a small television set, a keyboard, a mouse, and a box with a bunch of wires coming out of the back, right? To many people, that is all there is to a computer. To a programmer, however, that same computer is a gateway to a world where opportunities abound. The computer has the potential to become a tool to accomplish tasks. This potential is realized when a programming language is used to instruct the computer how the task is to be accomplished.

Programming languages provide the means for accomplishing two distinct purposes in relation to the computer: communication and guidance.

Communicating with the computer

Computer languages provide a way for humans to communicate with a computer. When a computer is running, an operating system — which, in itself, is a computer program — provides a way for users to enter commands that the computer translates and acts upon.

Computer languages allow interaction with the computer. For instance, say you wanted to move a computer file from one location to another on your hard drive. You could enter a command such as the following at the computer's command prompt:

```
move myfile.txt d:\oldfiles
```

This command may seem cryptic at first, but it is very straightforward — to the computer. Later in this chapter you will learn a bit about syntax, which defines how programming instructions are put together.

Guiding the computer

In reality, computers are dumber than a box of rocks. By themselves, they are nothing but a collection of wires running between electronic circuits. Fortunately, those circuits can be instructed to do certain things. Those instructions, when taken together, form computer programs.

Computer programs are different from computer commands, which I describe in the previous section. Commands are essentially individual in nature. They allow for real-time interaction between you and the computer. Programs, on the other hand, are a collection of commands designed so the computer can execute them in a specific order. Some programs are small, and others are huge — it all depends on the task being accomplished by the program.

The Tower of Babel

Just as computers are different, so are the languages in which they are programmed. The number of different languages used to program computers is astounding. Table 1-1 shows a sampling of the scores of different languages available. Remember that these are only the most popular languages; many others are more esoteric and less widely used.

Table 1-1:   Popular Computer Languages

Language	Comments
Assembly	Used for small programs
BASIC	Noted for ease of use
C	Powerful language used for many commercial programs
COBOL	Used for a vast array of business and financial programs on large and mid-size computers
Java	Popular on the World Wide Web and known for ability to run on a wide range of computer systems
Pascal	Highly structured and often used in educational environments

Language levels

Language understood directly by a computer is called *machine language.* This language consists of zeros and ones, which are understood directly by the computer's processor (the CPU). For instance, the following machine language programming instruction is a directive for an Intel Pentium CPU to add 23 to the eight-bit value in the accumulator:

```
00000100 00010111
```

If this sounds confusing, don't worry — it *is* confusing. That's why virtually no one programs in machine language. Instead, programming languages introduce different layers of abstraction into the process. This abstraction is necessary so programmers can more easily understand the commands they are giving the computer. For instance, in Assembly language, the following instruction has the same result as the previous machine language instruction:

```
ADD 23
```

The computer cannot understand this command directly. As you will learn in Chapter 2, intermediate programs convert this Assembly language statement into machine language, which the CPU can understand directly.

Assembly language is an example of a low-level language. This term simply means that there is a very close correlation between the commands used in the language and what those commands are translated into when they become machine language. In low-level languages, accomplishing tasks of any significance takes quite a few programming instructions.

High-level languages are much more abstract in their use of programming instructions. The commands used in high-level languages are closer to human language than they are to the machine language understood by computers. As an example, the following BASIC statement is relatively easy to understand:

```
A = B + 23
```

This line simply adds the value of 23 to whatever value is contained in the variable B and then assigns the result to the variable A. (Variables are nothing more than named values. You learn about variables in Chapter 6.)

Language versions

You already know that many different programming languages are available. Each programming language can also have many different versions. Languages are often adopted and adapted by a software publisher as they develop programming tools for use by developers.

Unfortunately, not all versions of a programming language are compatible with each other. If you write a program in one version of BASIC, for example, it might not be usable under a version of BASIC published by a different software publisher. Fortunately, a core set of instructions is typically compatible from one language version to another. If a programmer is developing a program that will need to be used under different versions of the same language, he or she will often write the program using only those core instructions.

Picking a Language

The number of programming languages available invariably leads to an overriding question on the part of many programmers: Which language should I use? This question can be answered in many ways. The following sections examine some of the factors that can affect your individual answer to this question.

Availability

Often, particularly when you are first starting out at programming, the question of which language to use is answered by what you have available at hand. Some operating systems come with one or more programming languages.

You can also download a free or shareware version of some languages from the Internet. A good way to look for these is by using a search engine, such as Yahoo!. Some of these products are limited versions or demos of full-featured products to which you can later upgrade.

Choosing a language strictly because it is available is not an entirely capricious decision. There is a pragmatic side as well. Programming languages tend to be rather expensive, and justifying the expense may be hard when you are just learning or you aren't sure you'll like the product. Thus, many people start out using whatever is available to them and then graduate to more full-featured or expensive programming environments as they learn more.

The availability issue is so persuasive — especially in a learning environment — that it led to the decision of which programming language to use for the examples in this book. Beginning in Chapter 4, you learn how to use a free version of BASIC that comes with Windows-based computers. That language version was selected simply because it is available to a majority of readers of this book.

Compatibility

One of the overriding concerns in your programming efforts may be the compatibility of your programs with those developed by others. For instance, you may find a program that is very close to what you need, and you can make it exactly right by modifying the *source code* (the programming instructions) just a little. In this case, you need to use the same language and version that was used to develop the code in the first place. Here, compatibility becomes the key factor in your language selection.

External mandates

Often the actual selection of a programming language is out of your control. You may be forced to select a particular language and version. This is most often the case at work, where the company may have standardized on a particular programming language long before you joined the organization. If you are developing software for use within a company, it is a good idea to find out if any policies are already in place concerning programming languages.

Strengths and weaknesses

Each computer language has its own strengths and weaknesses. Some languages are strong at processing algebraic formulas yet are weak when working with text. Others have many features that make working with text a snap but are not very good at working with files. The list could go on and on, but you get the idea.

No single computer language is good at every programming task. How do you find out the strengths and weaknesses of a particular language? The best way is to ask people that are already working with the language. What do they use? Why do they use it? What do they like about the language? What do they dislike? What do they wish it did better? You should, of course, tailor the questions to the tasks you seek to accomplish in your programming.

Understanding Syntax

You may have heard the term *syntax* before. It is nothing but a fancy way to describe how computer programming instructions or commands should be put together. Syntax is applicable to more than just computer languages — it is also applicable to human languages. English, for instance, has a rather loose syntax that defines how sentences should be constructed. For instance, a sentence should contain both a noun and a verb. Other pieces of grammar can be added to clarify or embellish the main thought of the sentence. If these elements are not present, or if they are not in the right order, then the sentence makes little sense. Consider the following:

```
Ran hill down quickly John the.
```

This sentence has all the proper words, but when they are out of order the meaning is either unclear or indecipherable. Other factors that can affect understanding are punctuation and capitalization. When the words are put in the proper order, punctuation is in the right place, and capitalization is correct, the sentence becomes meaningful and conveys the intended message. The following sentence uses the exact same words as the previous example, just in a different order:

```
John quickly ran down the hill.
```

This is the heart of syntax. You must use the proper words in the proper order following the proper construction rules in order to be understood. Computer languages are no different.

Elementary syntax

Believe it or not, the syntax rules followed by computers are not nearly as complex as those followed in human language. Programming commands (analogous to sentences) must be put together in exactly a certain way, or the tools that translate the commands into the computer's native machine language won't be able to do their job. They simply won't understand what is meant.

Most programming statements consist of one or two keywords, followed by one or more arguments. In some instances, there will also be an operator indicating exactly what is to take place. The number of keywords and operators is quite limited, but the arguments available can be quite extensive. Arguments are nothing more than modifiers that specify data to be used or specify the precise context that should be applied to the keyword itself.

One of the most elemental pieces of documentation for any programming language reference is a syntax guide. This is nothing more than an explanation of the command or keyword along with any possible arguments for that keyword. As you are learning a particular programming language, you will refer to such syntax guides often. (You can find them either in the printed language documentation or in the online help for the language.)

Differences between computer languages

Different languages have different syntaxes, however, which means that you must use the correct syntax when you perform similar operations using different languages. As an example, consider this very simple BASIC statement:

```
A = 1 + 2
```

This statement uses two operators (the equals and plus signs) and three arguments (the variable A and the numbers 1 and 2). It assigns the value of 1 + 2 to the variable A. Thus, when the statement is complete, the variable A will contain 3, which is the result of 1 + 2. The same statement in the C language looks like this:

```
A = 1 + 2;
```

Notice that it is very similar to the BASIC statement, with the addition of the semicolon at the end of the line because C requires a semicolon at the end of each statement. If the same simple addition statement is rendered in COBOL, it looks as follows:

```
COMPUTE a-var = 1 + 2
END-COMPUTE.
```

Here you can see quite a bit more difference between languages. The examples could continue on and on, but you get the idea — different languages do the same things differently. As you learn to work with one language and you are later called to work with another, you may need to learn an entirely new way of doing the tasks with which you are already familiar.

CHAPTER 2

DESIGN AND DEVELOPMENT ISSUES

IN THIS CHAPTER

- Deciding which programming platform to use
- Designing the right user interface
- Choosing a programming style

When you sit down to write a program, you must tackle several issues before you can begin the development process. This chapter discusses those issues. Here you learn why your programming platform is so important to the development process, why a great user interface can make or break your program, and how programming style can affect your development efforts.

Deciding on a Programming Platform

In computer terminology, a *platform* is a foundation on which a total computer system is built. To programmers, this foundation is created by two elements: hardware and operating system. The next sections examine these elements and how they affect your programming efforts.

How computer hardware affects your program

Computer hardware is the nuts and bolts of any computer system. When you work on a computer at home, school, or office, the computer hardware is the physical computer. You can touch hardware; it includes things like your keyboard, monitor, mouse, and the computer box itself.

Hardware has a huge impact on your programming efforts. The following items illustrate a few of the many ways that hardware affects how you program:

- The type of CPU (the computer brain) for which you're writing your program has a major effect on your program. If you're writing a program in a low-level language (such as Assembly language), you must write two completely different programs in order to use them on a Pentium CPU and a Motorola CPU, for example.

- Something as simple as a mouse can throw a complete monkey wrench into programming efforts. If you're writing a program for an IBM PC (or compatible) type of computer, you must write a program that accepts a two-button mouse because PCs always use this type of mouse. If you're writing a program for a Macintosh, your program must accept a one-button mouse, which is the Macintosh standard.

- The input devices on the computer for which you're writing a program affect your program. Some systems use keyboards for input, and others rely on joysticks or touch screens.

Clearly, you must understand the hardware on which your program will ultimately run before you can adequately create a program. Every program of any consequence is destined to receive input from some source (such as a keyboard, scanner, mouse, joystick, or touch screen), process that input in some way (this happens in the CPU), and then create output on some device (such as a monitor, printer, or hard drive). Thus, the most basic computer system functions are dependent on the hardware used for input, processing, and output. If you don't understand that hardware, you can't program for it.

How operating systems affect your program

Operating system is a generic term that describes the program (or collection of programs) used to operate computer hardware. Every computer system includes an operating system component. If you have a computer at home, chances are very good that it uses either the Windows operating system (developed by Microsoft) or a Macintosh operating system (developed by Apple Computer). These are the most common operating systems for small desktop computers.

Operating systems are used to control the various hardware elements that make up a computer. In reality, each operating system does essentially the same thing; they just go about it in an entirely different way.

Remember that operating systems are nothing but programs in their own right. Thus, programmers needed to write an operating system before you could use it on a particular computer. You, in turn, write your programs to take advantage of the programming code developed in the operating system.

As an example, consider the hard drive on your computer. This is a very common device for most computer systems. Files need to be stored on it, programs loaded from it, and data accessed. If you needed to write commands to write and read your information from the hard drive, your programming job would become much more tedious. Instead, the programmers who worked on the operating system wrote the commands to access the hard drive. These commands are then made available to your program as a group of functions. Accessing them is much easier than writing your own commands.

In computer terminology, collections of features you can access in an operating system are often called APIs, or Application Programming Interfaces. The computer language you use takes advantage of APIs to perform most of the mundane, yet very complex, tasks necessary on a computer.

As a programmer, you need to understand the operating system under which your program will run because different operating systems implement APIs in different ways. If you write a program that utilizes the Windows API, that same program will not work under UNIX or BeOS simply because the APIs on those systems are different.

Designing Your User Interface

When you know which platform your computer program will use, you need to consider a *user interface*. This is computer-speak for how your program interacts with its users. Typically, the user interface consists of two things: the on-screen appearance and the feedback mechanism.

On-screen appearance

You have probably used computer software before. Have you ever noticed that you can often tell what type of program you're using simply by glancing at the screen? This is because we have come to associate visual cues with particular types of programs or operating systems.

For instance, most people who see a program with a title bar, menu bar, and toolbar think about Windows programs (see Figure 2-1). This is not to say that programs for other operating systems don't use similar elements, but the *way* in which those elements appear gives us the impression that the program is running under Windows.

Figure 2-1: The on-screen appearance of a program often indicates the type of program it is.

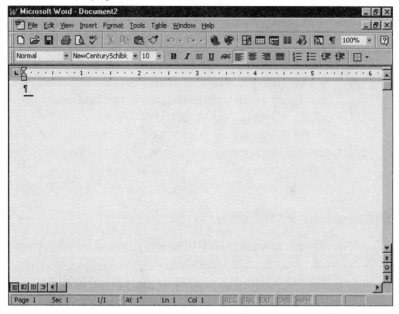

Your experiences with this recognition factor should teach an important lesson. Users come to expect a particular type of program to look a particular way. This familiarity engenders a certain comfort level with a program before it is even used. If you are writing a program for a particular platform, you should be familiar with how other programs on that platform appear. Your program should conform to user expectations concerning appearance. If it doesn't, users are less likely to use your program compared to similar (possibly competing) programs.

In general, two types of interfaces are commonly used in computer systems: textual and graphical. *Textual interfaces* are normally used with text-only displays. A *graphical user interface* (usually called a GUI, pronounced *gooey*) is much more complex than a textual interface. It relies on graphics, not just text, to display information. Graphics include pictures, graphs, charts, and other similar elements.

Feedback mechanisms

The heart of interacting with a user is the way in which those users provide commands and input to the program. The most elemental of these feedback mechanisms is a command line at which users enter words to instruct the program what to do next. Other feedback mechanisms include menus, toolbars, dialog boxes, status bars, and similar elements.

Users of programs on a particular programming platform very quickly become used to standard methods of program feedback. As a programmer, you need to be aware of what common feedback mechanisms are useful to and expected by users on a particular computing platform.

Picking a user interface

As you have already learned, the biggest determining factor in picking a user interface is the platform on which your program will run. Different platforms have developed different interface conventions over the years. This is not to say that you could not create a program that implements a different type of user interface. Doing so, however, runs the very real risk of alienating your users — a risk most programmers are not willing to take.

Fortunately, many programming environments provide easy ways to implement the most common user interfaces for your target platform. Chapter 3 introduces you to the different programming tools used in developing programs.

Choosing Your Programming Style

During the course of the past half-century, computer programmers have come up with a number of different solutions to computer programming problems. As you develop your own programs, you need to determine how you want to approach the problem of creating your own program. The following sections introduce three different programming approaches you can use: structured programming, modular programming, and object-oriented programming.

Structured programming

Perhaps the most elemental example of programming style is termed *structured programming*. This term simply means that the program uses structures to control the order in which programming instructions are performed. Most languages in use today employ programming commands that allow you to structure your program easily.

To understand how structured programming works, suppose that you want to go to town, and you prepare a shopping list to use. You place five items on your list and then start out on your trek. Instead of going from home to town five times (once for each item), you stay in town until you have picked up all the items. You could express your preparations and trip as follows:

```
make list
drive to town
while items remain on list
 (
  drive to new location in town
  pick up item
  cross item off list
 )
drive home
put items away
```

This example isn't written in any particular programming language. All it does is lay out the logic of your shopping trip. In this example, you repeat everything between the parentheses until the initial condition (`while items remain on list`) is met.

This example shows how a programming structure works. In such structures, you define a condition and then repeat a series of programming steps until that condition is met.

Modular programming

Most of today's programming languages allow you to also develop *modular programs*. This term simply means that you can break a program down into individual components that perform a set group of instructions. As an example, I'll revisit the idea of the shopping trip into town. You were so successful on your trip that you decide you want to start doing the same thing for other people. You sit by your phone, awaiting calls from friends and neighbors who will send you off into town with a new list of things to pick up.

Using the same sort of programming approach you previously used, you could express the completion of your tasks as follows:

```
while open for business
(
  sit by phone
  if phone rings
    (
    answer phone
    create new list
    hang up phone
    drive to town
    while items remain on list
      (
      drive to new location in town
      pick up item
      cross item off list
      )
    deliver items
    drive back home
    )
)
```

Notice that the procedure has become a bit more complicated. There are more decisions to be made. Notice, too, that there are three programming structures in the steps (as designated by parentheses), and they are nested within each other. (*Nesting* simply means that you do one programming structure while you are already doing another programming structure.)

You can imagine that as your day gets more complicated and you add more and more things to do, the expression of those tasks in a programming manner could get very complex. Here is where modular programming steps in. It allows you to break your tasks down into easy steps that can then be completed independently of the other tasks. For instance, in the example I just provided, you may view your main (highest-level) task as sitting by the phone and waiting for it to ring. In this case, your main program (the one you perform first) could be expressed as follows:

```
while open for business
(
 sit by phone
 if phone rings
  (
  handle call
  )
)
```

In this case, your program is much easier to understand and comprehend. All you have done is to move the bulk of the work to another module (called `handle call`) which is done only if the phone rings. Of course, you still need to write the module that defines what you do to actually handle the call. This could appear as follows:

```
handle call
answer phone
create new list
hang up phone
shop and deliver
```

Notice that this module can even call other modules, such as one that describes in great detail how to create a new list or the one called `shop and deliver`, which tells how to go to town, collect the desired items, and deliver them. When the `handle call` module is complete, you simply go up one level and continue what you were doing when the module was first started. (In this case, it means you go back to waiting for the phone to ring again.)

From a programming perspective, a modular approach to programming allows you to deal with smaller chunks of programming code rather than wade through huge listings. This approach is also helpful if there are multiple people on a programming team and each can be responsible for a particular module or group of modules. For instance, in the above example you could make someone else responsible for the `shop and deliver` module. You don't particularly care what happens inside the module, only that the expected results are done in a timely manner.

Object-oriented programming

The third approach to programming is *object-oriented programming* (OOP). It takes the concept of modular programming and pushes it to a new level. OOP allows the creation of well-designed modules that perform a particular task. These modules are also designed to be reusable, which means that they can be easily moved from one program to another.

In traditional programming, the data used by a program is kept separate from the programming code used to manipulate that data. All data is stored in one area of the computer's memory, and all the programming code is in another. If the data must change (for instance, you want to start tracking your mileage on your shopping trips), then the programs that access that data must also change. These changes can be troublesome, particularly if the program is quite large.

Object-oriented programming attempts to solve this problem by changing the fundamental way in which programs and data are stored in a computer. In OOP, the data is stored along with the program module used to initialize, access, and process that data. If another program module needs a piece of the data, it requests it from the module responsible for that data.

Changes to the data within a module are made available to other modules simply by changing the module responsible for the data. This eliminates the need to go through and change lots of different program locations, as is done under the modular or structured approaches to programming. The benefit to an organization is that programs are easier to maintain and modify in the long run.

CHAPTER 3

TOOLS FOR PROGRAMMING

- Using interpreters, compilers, and linkers
- Picking a programming environment
- Debugging
- Optimizing

Good craftspeople have a selection of tools that they can use to produce their wares. Programmers are no different. Their tools are not hammers, chisels, or brushes — they are the electronic equivalent of such traditional tools.

This chapter focuses on the primary tools you'll use in your programming efforts. In addition, you'll receive a crash course in how to use those tools and understand the tasks they perform.

Programming with Interpreters, Compilers, and Linkers

Chapters 1 and 2 explain that computers understand only their native language, called machine language. You write programs using programming languages, which are more easily understood by humans. But how do you turn your programming-language program into a machine-language program that a computer can understand? You use software tools called interpreters, compilers, and linkers. The following sections explain how these tools fit into the programming process.

Interpreting programming instructions

When you think of the term *interpreter,* you probably think of a person who translates speech or written words from one language to another, such as from English to German. Computer interpreters do pretty much the same thing — they take a program instruction written in one computer language and translate it to machine language. After the instruction is translated, the computer can act upon it.

As you enter your program in the language of your choice, you are putting together individual programming instructions. Interpreters take each instruction, do their magic, and pass the corresponding machine language to the CPU.

Interpreters are built into some programming environments. (You learn about programming environments later in this chapter.) They allow you to quickly see the results of a few instructions or a portion of your program. The downside, however, is that interpreters tend to be slow. This slowness is not a function of the translation process per se, but is related to the fact that the translation must be done every time the program is run.

How can you tell if your programming environment uses an interpreter? The easiest way to tell is if you are typing a program and you can click on a run button or issue a command that runs the program right away, starting the interpreter and resulting in the execution of your program instructions.

Compiling and linking programs

The alternative to interpreting your program is to use a compiler and linker. Whereas an interpreter needs to translate your program instructions to machine language every time you run the program, a compiler performs the translation all at once. It creates *object code,* which is stored in an *object module.* This is nothing but a disk file that contains the object code.

Object code is an intermediate form of a program that is not yet ready to be used. A *linker* is used to further process the object code. This programmer's tool combines the object code contained in several object modules into a final executable program. The CPU can use the machine language instructions in this program directly.

Understanding Programming Environments

The tools used by programmers, when taken as a whole, define a *programming environment*. This is simply a fancy way of looking at what programmers need to do and the tools they use to do it. There are two basic types of programming environments: integrated and non-integrated.

Using a non-integrated environment

Stand-alone programming tools characterize a non-integrated programming environment. The programming tools are used on their own as each is needed by the programmer. If you are using an interpreter for your programming, it is very rare to work in a non-integrated environment. These types of environments are common, however, if you are using a compiler and linker.

The primary advantage to a non-integrated programming environment is that the programmer has complete control over which tools are used. Tools from different vendors can be mixed and matched to create the desired overall environment.

Another advantage is that the programmer can more easily add different components to the environment. For instance, the programmer may learn about a new tool that promises to increase the efficiency of a program. In a non-integrated environment, adding such a tool to the mix without changing how work is done with the other tools is easy.

Using an integrated environment

An integrated programming environment attempts to combine all the common programming tools into a seamless working environment that puts everything at the programmer's fingertips. Figure 3-1 shows an example of this "one-stop shop" approach to programming environments.

In an integrated environment, the programmer uses the provided program editor to enter programming instructions and then uses the menus and toolbar buttons (if provided) to initiate the different tools available. The big advantage of integrated environments is that all the programming tools utilize the same user interface. Learning to use the tools is easier with each tool typically being only a button-click away.

Choosing an environment

Unfortunately, explicitly choosing a programming environment is not always easy. That choice is often made for you when you choose a programming language. For instance, if you want to program using Microsoft's Visual Basic, you're limited to an integrated environment; there are no other choices. Some languages, however, do provide choices. For instance, if you want to program in C, you have many different implementations to choose from. Some are integrated; some are not.

Figure 3-1: Visual Basic is an integrated programming environment.

Debugging Programs

Debugging is the process of removing errors (called *bugs*) from a program. Why are they there? Because programming is an error-prone process. The difficulty involved in getting rid of bugs will depend on many things: the complexity of your program, the data you are using, the design process you went through, and your temperament.

Many different types of bugs may creep into your programming code. Bugs typically fall into three categories:

■ **Syntax.** Just as grammar is important to ensuring that what you say is understood by other people, a computer language's syntax is vital in making sure the computer understands what you want done. Some languages catch and flag incorrect syntax as you enter a line of programming code. Other languages wait and display syntax errors when you execute the compiler. In either case, catching and fixing such errors is easy.

■ **Logic.** In computers, *logic* means the process and order in which tasks are accomplished. For instance, you may want your program to display information about the contents of a file. It appears that the records display properly, but for some reason, the subtotals don't come out right. Chances are good that this is a logic error — something is wrong in the code that is causing the wrong figures to add up.

■ **Operation.** These errors usually result from surpassing the limits of the tools you are using. For instance, say you have written a program and you exceed the storage capability of a variable or you attempt to do a division operation and the divisor is zero. These types of conditions result in incorrect data being used, and the second one will result in an error when it is encountered. These types of errors can be detected and compensated for, however, if you think through how your program will be used.

The effects of bugs can be devastating. For this reason it is in your best interest to find and fix bugs early in the development process. In general, the longer a bug remains undetected, the more costly it is to fix. This is why many programmers test their programs regularly as they are writing. If your program has a basic design flaw and you don't discover it until late in the development process, you may have to scrap the program and start over, which can be very expensive.

Taking precautions to avoid bugs

The best way to keep bugs out of your program is to take careful precautions to ensure that you never introduce a bug into the program in the first place. Developing good programming habits can aid you tremendously in keeping bugs out of your programs. The following precautions help you to avoid bugs:

- **Verify your design before starting.** If your program design is faulty to begin with, no amount of programming will fix the problem. Even though you are probably anxious to implement your ideas and start coding immediately, resist this temptation.

- **Keep program modules short.** As you are designing your program, do so with an eye toward modularity. Each module should perform one specific task — no more and no less.

- **Test as you go.** Much of your program code serves as a basis for later programming stages. By testing each module independently, you can isolate errors that are easier to fix while the code is still fresh in your mind.

- **Use meaningful variable names.** Chapter 6 shows you how to use variables. It is important to use variable names that are easily recognized. It is very easy to forget what variables like z or q7 are used for. It takes much less effort to recall the purpose of a variable called TotalTax or ReportTitle.

- **Add meaningful comments.** Every programming language provides a way for you to add comments to your program code. These comments are invaluable when you later examine your program to make changes.

Getting rid of bugs

Even if you exercise all the precautions mentioned earlier in this chapter, bugs will still manage to get through the cracks. You need to understand how to use the programming tools that you have available to remove bugs.

Different programming environments provide different types of tools you can use to uncover bugs. If you are using an integrated programming environment, chances are good that at least a few debugging tools are built right into the environment. If you are using a non-integrated environment, then the debugger is often a stand-alone program, or you must purchase such a debugger separately.

The debugging tools available to you as a programmer range from virtually nonexistent to quite complex. The following list describes a few of the more common tools:

- **Single-stepping:** *Single-stepping* enables you to step through your program one line at a time. While you step through your program, you can examine the value of different program variables or examine other settings to make sure that everything is working as expected.

- **Breakpoints:** Breakpoints are convenient because they enable you to execute your program up to a certain point at full speed. Then you can examine the value of variables and step a line (or a procedure) at a time to observe your program's behavior. If you use an interpreter, a breakpoint temporarily pauses your program, allowing you to probe memory and then continue from the point at which you paused (or *broke*) the running of the program. In a compiled environment, a breakpoint typically stops your program and displays the results of variables or other settings. Then you can examine the settings to look for any problems.

- **Memory dumps:** A *memory dump* is a debugging method that you can use in extreme cases of bug problems. You simply instruct your program to stop at a certain point and print its data to a disk file. Then you examine the data to find evidence of bugs.

Optimizing Programs

Optimize, at least in a programming context, is one of those nebulous terms whose true meaning is hard to tack down. Generally, it means to make something as good as it can be. Programs can be optimized in different ways. For instance, you could optimize a program for speed (the most common type of optimization) or you could optimize it for a particular hardware configuration. You could also optimize it for a particular type of data or for how you envision users using the program.

You, as programmer, must have a particular optimization goal in mind before you start on the quest of making your program better. The following sections cover some of the more common optimization goals, and the chapter finishes with a look at the optimization tools available to a programmer.

Optimizing for speed

Making a program operate as fast as it can is typically in a programmer's best interest. Thus, after a program is initially written, it is often desirable to go back, examine the code, and think of different ways to accomplish the same task more quickly.

At some point your program will be as fast as it can be. Unfortunately, for some applications, that still may not be fast enough. In those instances, you have only one option — rewrite the critical code in a faster language. This option often means picking a language such as Assembly language. Such a task can be very formidable and should be undertaken only if absolutely necessary.

Optimizing for size

In recent years, most computer software has been written as if there is unlimited hard disk space in the computer. It is not unusual to find software that requires 80MB of storage space.

Software doesn't have to be that way. You may have a goal to make your program as small as possible so it doesn't use a lot of disk space. For instance, you may have a goal of cramming your program onto a single high-density floppy disk.

Optimizing a program for size requires quite a bit of knowledge about how a particular language and compiler work. Some compilers include settings you can use to automatically optimize a program for size. These work because the compiler often has different ways it can translate your programming instructions into machine code. If you use the size optimization settings, the compiler will use the methods that require the least overall increase in size.

Optimizing for hardware

When you optimize your program for a particular hardware environment, you make some assumptions about your user. Primarily, you place requirements on what that user needs to run your program. For instance, you may require a particular type of hard drive, or a specific scanner. Your program can then be written to take advantage of that required hardware.

Perhaps the most common hardware optimization revolves around the CPU on which the program will run. Manufacturers often create CPUs in families, which is just a fancy way of saying that today's CPU will be superceded by a different, expanded version of the same CPU next year. That CPU will run programs designed for the earlier CPU. Thus, many programs are written so they will run on earlier CPUs. If you optimize your program to the later CPU, then it may run faster (because it takes advantages of the advances inherent to the new CPU), but you may also limit your market (because you exclude all those users with older CPUs).

Tools for optimizing

A whole thriving industry has grown up around the need for programmers to optimize their code. Many tools are available for you to use in your optimization pursuits. Primarily, the tools benchmark your program and produce reports that indicate how long your program takes to accomplish different tasks. (*Benchmarking* means that either your program faces a battery of standardized tasks to see how well it does or your program is simply timed while it is running.) Through the judicious use of these reports and examining your code, you can determine where you need to focus most of your attention.

To find optimization tools, examine any good programmers' product catalog or do a search on the Internet for optimization tools.

CHAPTER 4

GETTING TO KNOW THE BASIC PROGRAMMING ENVIRONMENT

IN THIS CHAPTER

- Understanding the variations of BASIC
- Installing QBasic
- Familiarizing yourself with the QBasic Environment

BASIC (an acronym for Beginner's All-purpose Symbolic Instruction Code) is one of the most popular computer languages. This chapter introduces you to the basics of BASIC. After a quick waltz through the different variations of BASIC, you get your feet wet by beginning to use QBasic, a version of BASIC available to everyone using a Windows-based PC.

Understanding the Variations of BASIC

More variations of BASIC probably exist than any other computer programming language in history. The following are just a few of the different variations of BASIC available:

- **Chipmunk Basic.** This is a freeware BASIC interpreter for the Macintosh. You can find more information about Chipmunk Basic at www.rahul.net/rhn/cbas.page.html.

- **FutureBASIC.** One of the premiere BASIC programming environments for the Macintosh. You can visit the FutureBASIC Web site at www.stazsoftware.com.

- **QBasic.** The last version of BASIC created by Microsoft for the DOS world. This is an interpreted version of BASIC without a whole lot of bells and whistles.

- **QuickBASIC.** The same as QBasic, but with a compiler. This allows you to create stand-alone programs that can be run from the DOS prompt.

- **True BASIC.** The commercial version of the original BASIC language. The creators of BASIC (John Kemeny and Thomas Kurtz) are the founders of the company. Versions exist for Windows, Macintosh, OS/2, and UNIX/Linux systems. You can visit the True BASIC Web site at www.truebasic.com.

- **Visual Basic.** This is the Windows-centric descendant of QuickBASIC. Microsoft brought out the earliest Visual Basic in the early days of Windows and has been enhancing it ever since.

Understand that these are not all the versions of BASIC available. Dozens of them are each carving out their own little niche in the programming world. You can find versions of BASIC for almost any operating system and hardware platform that you can think of.

This book assumes you have access to a Windows-based computer, so you'll learn how to create your first programs by using QBasic. This flavor of BASIC is an interpreted version of the language (as I discuss in Chapter 2), so it is easy to use. Before you know it, you'll be creating programs without a second thought!

Installing QBasic

QBasic is not automatically installed when you install Windows, but it is available on the original Windows CD-ROM. Unless you have installed it before, it is *not* on your computer.

If you think it may already be installed, you can follow these steps:

1. Click the Start button. Windows displays the Start menu.

2. Choose Start➪Programs. Windows displays the Programs menu.

3. Click the MS-DOS Prompt option. (If you're using Windows NT, it's the Command Prompt option.) Windows opens a small command prompt window, awaiting your input.

4. Type **QBasic** (it doesn't matter if it is upper- or lower-case) and press Enter.

At this point, if you see a message welcoming you to QBasic (see Figure 4-1), you know that it is installed and you can skip the rest of this section. If you instead see an error message (such as "Bad command or file name"), then you know it is not installed.

If QBasic is not installed on your system, it is very easy to install. In fact, QBasic installation is much easier than most Windows-based programs. To install QBasic, follow these steps:

1. Insert your Windows CD-ROM in your CD-ROM drive. Depending on how your version of Windows is configured, you may or may not see a dialog box offering to install Windows. If this dialog box does appear, simply close it. You don't want to install Windows, just QBasic.

2. Click the Start button. Windows displays the Start menu.

3. Choose Start➪Programs. Windows displays the Programs menu.

Figure 4-1: QBasic can be run in a small command prompt window.

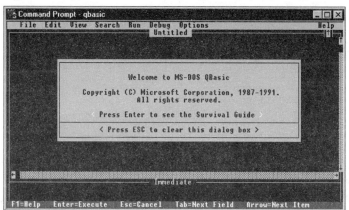

4. Click Windows Explorer. (If you're using Windows NT, it's the Windows NT Explorer option.) Windows opens the familiar Explorer window shown in Figure 4-2.

5. In the left side of the Explorer window, click the plus sign (+) to the left of the icon for your CD-ROM drive. The folders on the CD-ROM appear directly underneath the CD-ROM drive's icon.

6. Click the plus sign that appears to the left of the Tools folder. The Tools folder is among those that appeared when you performed Step 5. When you click the plus sign, another list of folders appears directly underneath the Tools folder.

7. Click the icon for the Oldmsdos folder. The folder opens and the contents of the folder appear in the right side of the Explorer window, as shown in Figure 4-3.

8. Select the two QBasic files in the right side of the Explorer window. You can select both files by holding down the Ctrl key as you click on each of them with the mouse.

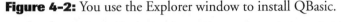

Figure 4-2: You use the Explorer window to install QBasic.

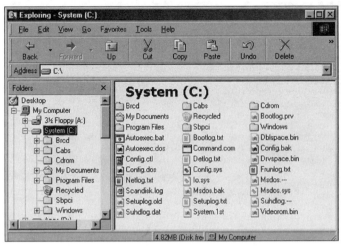

9. Click the plus sign that appears to the left of the Windows folder in the left portion of the Explorer window. You may need to explore a bit to find the Windows folder. It is typically on the C: drive, which is under the My Computer hierarchy in the Explorer. When you click on the plus sign, a number of folders appear under the Windows folder. One of these folders is called Command.

10. Move the mouse over one of the selected QBasic files in the right side of the Explorer window and click the mouse button.

11. Drag the QBasic files to the left side of the Explorer window, highlighting the Command folder you located in Step 9.

12. Release the mouse button. Explorer copies the two QBasic files to the Command folder on your hard drive.

You have now installed QBasic — all it took was copying two simple files to your hard drive.

Figure 4-3:   The Oldmsdos folder contains the QBasic files.

QBasic Program file

QBasic Help file

Oldmsdos folder is selected

Note that even though QBasic is installed on your system, it does not appear within the Start menu hierarchy, as do Windows-based programs. That is because QBasic is a DOS program, and they do not appear on the menus, by default. You can still run QBasic at any time you desire, however.

When you are done installing QBasic, you can remove the Windows CD-ROM and place it back in its storage location.

Starting QBasic

With the QBasic files installed on your system, you're ready to start the program and begin using the programming environment. You can start QBasic in two ways. The method you use is entirely up to you. The first method is as follows:

1. Click the Start button. Windows displays the Start menu.

2. Click the Run option from the Start menu. Windows displays the Run dialog box.

3. In the Open box, type **QBasic**. It doesn't matter if you use upper- or lowercase characters.

4. Click on the OK button or press Enter. Windows runs QBasic and displays a small Microsoft QuickBASIC dialog box. (Remember that QuickBASIC and QBasic are very similar; one evidence of this is the misnamed dialog box.) This dialog box allows you to enter parameters to affect how QBasic operates. You don't need to enter any such parameters for your purposes.

5. Press Enter or click the OK button. The QBasic dialog box disappears and the QBasic program screen fills the screen.

You are now ready to use QBasic, without any further ado. QBasic is running in full-screen mode, which is a special operating mode for Windows. When QBasic is in this mode, nothing else appears to be running on your computer. This is not true; Windows is still running. To switch to a different Windows program, press Ctrl+Esc at any time. To later switch back to QBasic, click the QBasic icon on the Windows taskbar.

If you want to run QBasic in a regular window on your desktop, use the second method of starting the program. This method uses the same steps as the testing you did earlier in the chapter to see if QBasic was installed:

1. Click the Start button. Windows displays the Start menu.

2. Choose Start⇨Programs. Windows displays the Programs menu.

3. Click the MS-DOS Prompt option. (If you're using Windows NT, it's the Command Prompt option.) Windows opens a small command prompt window and awaits your input.

4. Type **QBasic** (it doesn't matter if it is upper- or lower-case) and press Enter.

At this point, the QBasic welcome screen appears. The only difference is that when you use this method of starting QBasic, the program window appears small, taking up only a portion of your desktop (see Figure 4-1). To expand the window to fill most of your desktop, simply click on the Maximize button in the upper-right corner of the program window.

Understanding the QBasic Interface

When the QBasic welcome screen appears, you can press the Esc key to get rid of the welcome message and get down to business. At this point, you are faced with the QBasic program screen (see Figure 4-4), which you may find intimidating.

I describe each part of the program screen (menus, status line, Program window, and Immediate window) in this section. If you aren't familiar with DOS program interfaces, then you may find the QBasic interface a bit lacking when compared with traditional Windows-based programs. All the elements of a good interface are there, however, even if they are created with text and not with the fluid graphics you may be more familiar with.

Figure 4-4: The QBasic program screen

The QBasic menus

At the top of the QBasic program screen is a series of menus. These menus allow you to select different options that affect how QBasic interacts with you or runs the program you are working on. You will use many of these menu options through the course of this book. The menu choices are as follows:

- **File.** This menu option includes choices that allow you to load, save, and print program files.

- **Edit.** The choices available through this menu option allow you to do traditional editing tasks, such as cutting, copying, and pasting. You can also use this menu option to create new modules, which you learn about in Chapter 8.

- **View.** Only three choices are available through this menu option. They allow you to view any procedures you have defined, split the Program window (which I describe shortly) into two parts, and look at any output from your program.

- **Search.** The choices available through this menu option allow you to conduct searches for information and make replacements.

■ **Run.** This menu controls the execution of your program. It allows you to run, restart, or continue running your program. (You continue running a program after you pause it for debugging purposes.)

■ **Debug.** In Chapter 3, you learned that programmers need to debug their programs. The choices under this menu option provide you with tools to do so.

■ **Options.** This menu option provides a way to customize a few of the features available within QBasic. I discuss these options later in this chapter.

■ **Help.** This option is all the way at the right side of the line on which the menus appear. The choices available through this menu option allow you to access the information in the QBasic Help file on your system.

You can use the menus by either clicking on them with the mouse pointer or by pressing the Alt key and the highlighted menu character. Note that the menus are not activated and no menu characters are highlighted until you press the Alt key the first time. If you change your mind and want to go back to working on your program, pressing the Esc key cancels any menu selections in progress.

The status line

At the bottom of the screen is a status line. It is used primarily to indicate some of the keys you can press to perform common actions. For instance, if you look at Figure 4-4, notice that the status line includes the characters <F5=Run>. This simply means that if you press the F5 key, QBasic runs the program you are developing. Other keys are also indicated on the status line.

The Program window

The majority of the QBasic program screen is consumed by the Program window. This area is initially headed by the word "Untitled" (see Figure 4-4). The Program window is where (oddly enough) your program is listed. It is where you type your program and where you will do most of your work in this book.

The word "Untitled," which appears at the top center of the Program window, is only there when you first start QBasic or if you are working on a brand-new (unnamed) program file. After you save your program file, or if you load a program file from disk, "Untitled" changes to the name of your program.

The Immediate window

The bottom portion of the QBasic program screen is headed by the word "Immediate." This part of the screen is called the Immediate window, and it is a place where you can type commands that are immediately interpreted and acted upon by QBasic. You will use this window a lot when you debug your program.

To activate the Immediate window, click in it with the mouse pointer. You can also press F6 to switch back and forth between the Program and Immediate windows.

Setting Environment Options

QBasic provides you with a few options that you can modify in order to customize how the program screen appears. These options are accessible by using the Options menu. The three choices visible when you select the Options menu allow you to control the following items:

- **Display.** This option allows you to change the colors used to display information within QBasic.

- **Help Path.** This option allows you to specify where the QBasic Help file is located. You should not have to change this option.

- **Syntax Checking.** This option controls whether QBasic checks each of your program lines as you enter them to see if you used the proper syntax. This can be a great help while you are programming.

Exiting QBasic

When you are done with a programming session, you'll want to exit the QBasic program. You do so by choosing File⇨Exit. If you were working on a program and you did not save your changes, QBasic asks you if you want to save them before exiting.

CHAPTER 5

WRITING A SIMPLE PROGRAM

IN THIS CHAPTER

■ Entering your program

■ Running your program

■ Changing program lines

■ Saving your program

By now, you should feel fairly comfortable with the QBasic environment, first introduced in the previous chapter. Now it's time to enter and run your first program. This chapter covers exactly how you do that, using a very simple program. When you're done working through this chapter, you'll understand how to enter, change, and run a program.

Don't worry — it isn't as difficult as it sounds. In fact, QBasic makes it very easy to enter your program and get started.

Typing Your Program in QBasic

When you program in QBasic, you enter each line of the program in the Program window. All you need to do is type, and QBasic takes care of the rest. To see how to enter lines of your program, type the following in the Program window:

```
print
```

Now, press Enter to signify that you are done entering the program line. Each line in your program begins on a new line on-screen, and you signify the end of a program line by pressing Enter. When you do, QBasic examines your line and recognizes what you entered as a *keyword*. Each program line must contain at least one keyword. These keywords are commands that tell QBasic what you want to do.

In this case, the single word you entered is the keyword. QBasic changes the keyword to uppercase as soon as you press Enter. (See Figure 5-1.) QBasic always converts keywords to uppercase so they can be easily distinguished from other words in your program.

Figure 5-1:   QBasic converts keywords into uppercase characters.

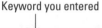

Keyword you entered

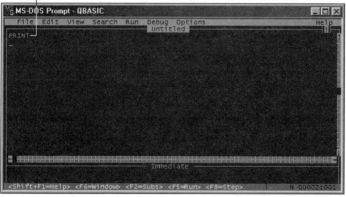

The PRINT keyword is a commonly used command to display something on the screen. When QBasic executes the program line, PRINT causes a blank line to print on the screen.

The cursor should be positioned on the line directly beneath the single line you just entered. You're ready to enter the second line of your program. Enter the second line just as you see it here:

```
Print "Hello World"
```

Notice that when you again press Enter at the end of the line, QBasic recognizes PRINT as a keyword and makes it all uppercase. Observe, however, that everything within the quotation marks was left exactly as you entered it. QBasic considers that to be a *string* (a series of characters) that you want left "as is."

Notice the use of the PRINT keyword in this, the second line of your program. Here you specified, right after PRINT, what you wanted to print. When QBasic executes the program line, it will display on-screen the text within the quotation marks. The marks themselves are not displayed; just the text within them.

Now, enter the third line of your program. Enter the following, exactly as you see it here:

```
prnt
```

When you press Enter, notice that QBasic acts a bit differently than when you entered the previous lines. In this case, the line was not converted to uppercase because QBasic could not locate a keyword on the line. As you get more adept at using QBasic, you'll pick up on these little clues as indicators that something is wrong and needs to be corrected. In this case, simply use the keyboard arrow keys to go back up and insert the letter *i* between the *r* and the *t*. When you move the cursor off the line, QBasic recognizes *print* as a keyword and formats it accordingly.

You have three more lines to enter in your program. Go ahead and enter them now:

```
PRINT "I hope things are going well today!"
PRINT "This is my first program"
END
```

These lines just print some additional text on the screen. The final line uses the END keyword to signify to QBasic that the end of the program has been reached.

When you have entered all six lines of your program, your screen should look like what you see in Figure 5-2.

Figure 5-2: Your first QBasic program is complete.

Your program doesn't look like a whole lot; after all, it is only six short lines. However, the process you used in writing those six lines is exactly the same process that programmers use in developing programs that use millions of lines. In both cases, you type a line, press Enter, and then type the next line. You continue doing this until you've entered all the lines you need to complete your program.

Running Your Program

You have now finished your program and are ready to run it. *Running* a program means that you tell QBasic you want to execute the commands you have collected together to form your program. You can run your new program by pressing F5, pressing Shift F5, choosing Run⇨Run, choosing Run⇨ Continue, or entering the RUN command in the Intermediate window.

The method you choose to run your program is entirely up to you, but most QBasic programmers find the F5 key to be the easiest way to remember and use (particularly since it appears on the status line at the bottom of the QBasic program screen).

It is interesting to note that there is no difference in effect between Run and Continue when you are first starting a program. If, on the other hand, you're debugging a program, there is a big difference between the two commands. The Run command always begins at the beginning of a program, whereas Continue simply starts up where you last paused the program.

Regardless of how you run your program, QBasic quickly displays the results, as shown in Figure 5-3. (Congratulations! You are now a programmer.) These results are shown on what is called the QBasic Output window. It's a DOS screen that shows the results of executing your program statements.

Figure 5-3: The results of running your first QBasic program

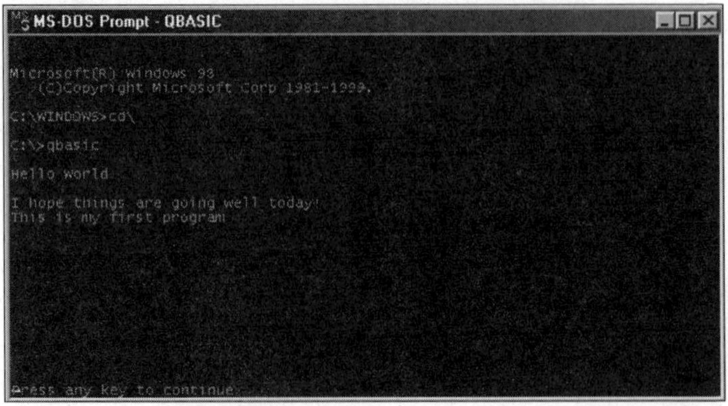

```
MS-DOS Prompt - QBASIC                                    _ □ ×

Microsoft(R) Windows 98
    (C)Copyright Microsoft Corp 1981-1999.

C:\WINDOWS>cd\

C:\>qbasic

Hello World

I hope things are going well today!
This is my first program





Press any key to continue
```

Notice that your Output window may also contain additional information, as is the case in Figure 5-3. This information is the remnants of any programs or commands that were executed before you ran your program. In the next section, you can discover how to clean up the Output window so that nothing else except your program output is displayed.

At the bottom of the Output window, notice the `Press any key to continue` message. This is a notification that the program is done running and you should press a key when you are done looking at the output. When you do press a key, QBasic again displays the program screen.

Editing Your Program

When you know how to enter a program, you essentially also know how to change one: Move the cursor in the Program window to the place where you want to make the change and then proceed to do so. In many ways, this process is much like using a simple word processor. The difference is that your words are keywords and data, and your sentences are program statements.

To see how to make changes, move the cursor to the beginning of the program. Change the first line to the following:

```
cls
```

When you type this, notice that the existing characters on the line (`PRINT`) move to the right. You can press the Delete key to remove them from your program. When you are done, move your cursor to the second line by pressing the ↓ key. QBasic recognizes the new keyword and capitalizes it as CLS.

The CLS keyword is shorthand for "clear screen." It does exactly that — it clears the screen and positions the output cursor in the upper-left corner of the screen. By placing this command at the beginning of your program, you inform QBasic that you want to start the program with a clean slate (always a good idea).

Run your program again to see what output is now produced. Your screen should appear similar to what you see in Figure 5-4.

Figure 5-4: You can cause QBasic to clear the screen when running your program.

A second look at the print statement

Now you'll make a few more changes in your program so you can understand a bit more about how QBasic works. First, change the fifth line of your program so it looks like the following:

```
PRINT "This is my second program"
```

This simple change will slightly modify what QBasic displays when the program is executed. Before running the program, however, add a semicolon to the end of the fourth program line. It should appear as follows:

```
PRINT "I hope things are going well today!";
```

Now when you run your program, the output is quite a bit different from what you saw previously (see Figure 5-5). Notice that the output from the fourth and fifth lines of the program is squished together on a single line.

Figure 5-5: Adding a simple semicolon to a PRINT statement can make a big difference.

I say "squished together" because there is no space after the exclamation point. Believe it or not, this is normal behavior for QBasic.

Normally, the PRINT statement does its work by including a carriage return and line feed at the end of what it prints. In other words, PRINT moves the cursor to the beginning of the next line of output. The semicolon you added at the end of the fourth program line changed everything, however. It informed QBasic that you didn't want to terminate the line. Instead, you wanted the PRINT statement to leave the cursor right at the end of the line. Therefore, when the next PRINT statement (in the fifth line of the program) was executed, it started its output right where the previous PRINT statement ended up.

Dealing with errors

QBasic recognizes many types of errors itself. When such an error is detected, you are informed of the fact and you can make a change to correct the error. To see how this works, take a look at your program as it now appears in the QBasic Program window:

```
CLS
PRINT "Hello World"
PRINT
PRINT "I hope things are going well today!";
PRINT "This is my second program"
END
```

You already know that this program runs without any problems. Let's add a few more lines, however, that have some purposeful errors in them. Add the following lines just before the END statement. Make sure you type them exactly as you see them here. All you need to do is position the cursor at the beginning of the END statement and start typing.

```
prin
PRINT "Programmers do interesting work throughout
the day.
```

You may have noticed a couple of things as you entered these two lines. When you entered the first line, QBasic didn't format the line as a keyword because you misspelled the word — a very common occurrence. Even though you didn't put a closing quotation mark at the end of the second line, though, QBasic figured you made a mistake and provided one for you as soon as you pressed the Enter key. (This is one way that QBasic helps to compensate for simple oversights and errors.)

Now run your program. If you typed the program lines exactly as shown above, you should see an error message on your screen, as shown in Figure 5-6. The reason for this is that QBasic looked at the program line and couldn't recognize any keywords.

Figure 5-6:   QBasic questions you when you may have made a mistake.

You'll probably see these types of notifications often, particularly as you're learning the ropes of QBasic. Notice that QBasic highlights the offending line and displays the message indicating what type of error it discovered. To correct the error, click OK or press Enter and then change the program statement containing the error.

Performing lots of changes

As you use QBasic more, your programs will inevitably get longer. After a short time, they'll be too long to fit on the screen and you'll need to use the scroll bars to display different sections of the program.

When your programs get this long, making changes can be challenging — particularly if a lot of them need to be made. Fortunately, QBasic includes a search and replace feature that can help make the changes for you.

To search for something in your program, choose Search➪Find. QBasic asks you to indicate what you want to find, as shown in Figure 5-7.

Figure 5-7: You can search for items quickly by using QBasic's Find command.

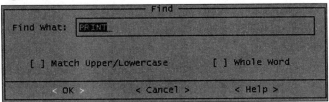

The default search word, provided as a courtesy by QBasic, is whatever word the cursor was on when you selected the Find option from the Search menu. You can change the Find What field to anything you like. The options at the bottom of the dialog box allow you to limit what QBasic considers a match.

After providing your search specifications, click on OK. QBasic highlights the first match it locates in your program. You can then make any changes you desire and press F3 to find the next match.

If you want QBasic to make changes for you, use the Change option from the Search menu. In this case, QBasic prompts you for not only what to find, but also what to replace it with, as shown in Figure 5-8.

Figure 5-8: QBasic allows you to easily replace items in your program.

```
┌─────────────────────── Change ───────────────────────┐
│ Find What: [                                        ] │
│                                                       │
│ Change To: [                                        ] │
│                                                       │
│   [ ] Match Upper/Lowercase      [ ] Whole Word       │
│ < Find and Verify > < Change All > < Cancel > < Help >│
└───────────────────────────────────────────────────────┘
```

If you are not sure whether every instance of the specified text should be changed, you can click on Find and Verify.

QBasic finds the first instance and you can change it or ignore it as you desire. For instance, Figure 5-9 shows the results of searching for DAY in the program and then clicking on Find and Verify.

Figure 5-9:   The Change option asks you to check out a proposed change.

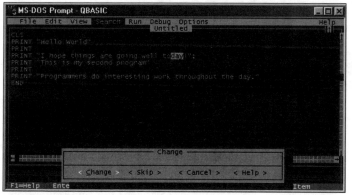

Saving Your Work on Disk

After a long day of working on your program, you probably want to save your work so you don't have to type it all in again later. (Actually, don't wait until the end of the day. Save your work periodically so it is safe on your disk drive.)

To save your work, choose File⇨Save. Because this is the first time you are saving your program, QBasic asks you to specify a file name, as shown in Figure 5-10.

Figure 5-10: You must provide a file name for your program.

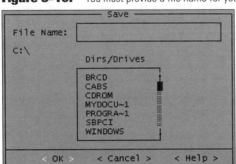

When you input a file name, keep it short. The name should be no longer than eight characters. Remember that QBasic is a DOS program and therefore follows DOS file naming conventions. You don't need to specify a file name extension (a period followed by up to three characters) — QBasic assumes you want to use .BAS as your file name extension.

In this instance, pick a drive and directory for your program and then use the name MYPROG. Type that in the File Name box and then click OK. The file is saved on your disk drive. Now, whenever you choose File⇨Save, the program is automatically saved using the same file name you just specified.

CHAPTER 6

USING DATA IN YOUR PROGRAM

IN THIS CHAPTER

- Understanding data types
- Using variables
- Using constants
- Using operators

Computers are very good at manipulating data. *Data* is nothing more than information stored in an organized manner. Any programming language allows you to store data and perform operations using that data.

Understanding how data is used in a program is vital to effective programming. I cannot stress this point enough. To understand exactly how to use QBasic in the subsequent chapters, you must understand the information about data, variables, and constants presented in this chapter.

Toward the end of this chapter, you also learn about operators. These are the tools that allow you to use the data in your program in new and exciting ways. They, in effect, allow you to process or change your data to any new form you desire.

Using Data Types

QBasic allows you to work with several different types of data. The fact that data can be categorized into types is essential for the efficient operation of QBasic and any programs you create. Each data type has different characteristics; each is matched to handling a specific type of data. QBasic supports the following data types:

- **Integer.** Integers are typically used for any programming purpose where a small number will do. Integers are whole numbers, such as 1, 2, 3, and so on.

- **Long.** The long data type is used anywhere you would normally use an integer, but the integer data type would not be sufficient to hold a large enough value. If you had to count to a million, an integer wouldn't do, but a long data type would be more than sufficient.

- **Single.** The single data type can be used to represent very large negative or positive real numbers (those that include something to the right of the decimal point). Because singles can be so huge, QBasic allows you to specify the numbers using scientific notation.

- **Double.** The double data type works the same way as the single data type, but it is used to represent numbers that need quite a bit more precision.

- **String.** Much of the data used in a program does not represent numeric values. In the previous chapter, you learned about strings as you developed your first program. A string is nothing more than a group of characters and is denoted by surrounding the string with quote marks.

Different languages support different data types. QBasic's support of these five data types doesn't mean that they are used in a different language or even in a different version of BASIC. If you go on to use a programming language other than QBasic, you need to research and learn which data types are used in that language.

Understanding Variables

You probably already know that computers store information in memory. *Variables* are storage places set aside in memory for the purpose of saving a particular data value. It sometimes helps to think of variables as a named container for values. These containers are called variables because their contents can vary.

Variables are powerful because they allow you to create general-purpose program statements that can act and make decisions based on the values within the variables. For instance, consider the following logical sentence:

If I have enough money, I will go on a date tonight.

In this instance, money is the variable. If you have enough, you will do something; if not, you won't. Variables serve the same purpose in your computer programs.

Declaring variables

Before you can use variables in your program, you must declare them. This declaration can be either implicit or explicit. You can either formally declare your variables (explicit) or you can informally declare them (implicit) by just using them.

If you are developing a short program, you typically use implicit declarations. Consider the following short program:

```
CLS
A% = 27
B$ = "John"
PRINT B$;
PRINT "is";
PRINT A%;
PRINT "years old."
END
```

You may recognize many of the elements of this program; it uses most of what you learned in Chapter 5. The second and third lines are where the variables are declared; the next four lines are where they are put to work. The output of this program is shown in Figure 6-1.

Figure 6-1: Variables can be used to display information in QBasic.

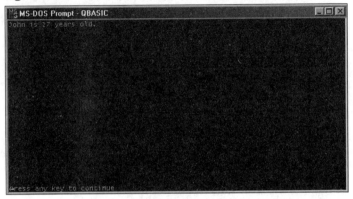

This program uses two variables: A% and B$, both of which are implicitly declared when they are first used. These variables consist of two different parts. The first is the variable name, in this case A and B. The second is the suffix, in this case % and $. The variable names can be up to 40 characters in length. Thus, you could use names such as MyVar or FridayAmount. Variable names cannot contain any spaces, nor should they be the same as any of the QBasic keywords.

The suffix you use with your variable name informs QBasic of what data type it should use for the variable. In this case, the % suffix means that the variable A is an integer data type. Table 6-1 shows the different suffixes you can use to declare your variables.

Table 6-1:   Suffixes Used to Denote Data Types

Data Type	Suffix	Example
Integer	%	MyCounter%
Long	&	GrandmaAge&
Single	!	FamilyDebt!
Double	#	MoneyInBank#
String	$	ClientName$

When you write longer programs, you'll want to explicitly declare your variables. If you get into the habit of explicitly declaring your variables, it becomes much easier to see how data is used in your program. As an example of explicitly declaring variables, consider the following short program:

```
CLS
DIM MyName AS STRING
MyName = "Allen Wyatt"
PRINT "My name is ";
PRINT MyName
END
```

The second line of the program is where the actual variable declaration takes place. Notice that the declaration uses the DIM keyword. This is shorthand for *dimension,* which simply means that QBasic sets aside memory for the variable used in the statement. In this case, the variable MyName is declared using the string data type. Whenever you declare your variables using this approach, you can declare them as integer, long, single, double, or string.

Assigning values to variables

You have already learned how to initially assign values to variables — by using the equals sign in an equation. To assign a string to a variable, surround the string with quote marks.

The following program line assigns the characters `Boiled Cabbage` to the variable `BluePlate$`:

```
BluePlate$ = "Boiled Cabbage"
```

Note that the quote marks are not part of the resulting variable string. They are only used to inform QBasic where the string begins and ends.

Variables retain their values until you assign some other value to them. You can see this effect in the following program:

```
CLS
DIM MyVar AS INTEGER
MyVar = 14
PRINT "MyVar is now"; MyVar
MyVar = 32
PRINT "MyVar is now"; MyVar
MyVar = 5
PRINT "MyVar is now"; MyVar
END
```

During the course of this program, the integer variable `MyVar` contains three different values: 14, 32, and 5. The results of running the program are shown in Figure 6-2.

Using variable arrays

QBasic also supports the use of variable arrays. *Arrays* are a way for you to keep related information together. For instance, say you're a teacher and you're working on a program to track information (names, grades, and so on) about your students. Because the student names are composed of text characters, the variables used to store the names should be strings. However, using a different string for each student name could quickly become cumbersome. Instead, you can use a variable array for the student names. If you have seven students in your class, you can assign them to an array as follows:

Figure 6-2: You can vary the information stored in variables.

```
Student$(1) = "Davis, John"
Student$(2) = "Morris, Judy"
Student$(3) = "Peterson, Becky"
Student$(4) = "Quillen, Terry"
Student$(5) = "Rongel, Bruce"
Student$(6) = "Thompson, Kerri"
Student$(7) = "Vickersly, Vance"
```

Note the *subscripts* (in parentheses) after each of the variable suffixes. These subscripts allow QBasic to tell each instance of Student$ apart. In programming terminology, each subscript represents a different *element* of Student$. In this case, Student$ has a single dimension consisting of seven elements.

If the array you are using in your program has more than ten elements or more than one dimension, you must explicitly declare it. You declare arrays by using the DIM statement you are already familiar with. Either of the following forms can be used to declare your array:

```
DIM SmallArray%(25)
DIM BigArray(499,2,3) AS STRING
```

In this instance, SmallArray% is an integer array with one dimension and BigArray is a string array with three.

Understanding Constants

Variables aren't the only type of data you can use in your program. QBasic also allows you to use constants. The only difference between constants and variables is that the value of variables can vary and the value of constants cannot. (That makes sense, right?)

Constants must be explicitly declared. They can be used in your program exactly the same as you use variables. Typically, constants are used when you want to use a symbolic name to refer to a value and you don't want the value to ever change.

You declare constants by using the CONST keyword rather than the DIM keyword. You also assign a value to the constant at the same time you declare it. For instance, the following short program uses a single constant named UserName:

```
CLS
CONST UserName = "Fred Johnson"
PRINT "The user name is "; UserName
END
```

You may also have noticed that you don't have to include data type suffixes with constants as you do with variables. Instead, QBasic simply takes what you assign to the constant and substitutes it for any occurrence of the constant name later in your program.

Understanding Operators

So far you have learned how you can assign values to variables directly by using the equals sign. QBasic also provides a wide range of operators that allow you to perform operations on the values in your variables. The following sections detail the operators at your disposal.

Math operators

The most common types of operations are those involving the use of math. These operations include the ones you use in everyday life, although QBasic throws in a few obtuse operators as well. Table 6-2 details the different math operators you can use.

Table 6-2: The QBasic Math Operators

Operator	Meaning
+	Addition
-	Subtraction
*	Multiplication
/	Division
^	Exponentiation
\	Integer division
Mod	Modulus

The four basic math operations (addition, subtraction, multiplication, and division) are fairly straightforward. The following short listing shows how such operators can be used in a program:

```
CLS
DIM Num1 AS SINGLE
DIM Num2 AS SINGLE
DIM Result AS SINGLE
Num1 = 213.17
Num2 = 78.3
PRINT "Result is now"; Result
Result = Num1 - Num2
PRINT "Result is now"; Result
Result = Result * 4.21 / Num1
PRINT "Result is now"; Result
END
```

The output from this program is shown in Figure 6-3. The first line of output shows that Result begins with a value of zero because nothing has yet been assigned to the variable. Your program then informs you that if you subtract 78.3 (Num2) from 213.17 (Num1), you get 134.87 (Result); if you multiply that Result by 4.21 and divide by 213.17 (Num1), you get 2.663615 (the new Result).

Figure 6-3: QBasic provides operators that allow you to perform common math operations.

Notice from the last equation in the program (Result = Result * 4.21 / Num1) that you can mix the use of literals (the number 4.21) and variables in the same equation. You can also use the Result variable on both sides of the equals sign to produce a desired outcome. This versatility allows you to quickly and easily put together any type of equation you need.

You may sometimes need to multiply a number by itself. Exponentiation is a shorthand method of multiplying a number repeatedly. For instance, $4 * 4$ is written as $4 \wedge 2$ and pronounced as "four raised to the second power." Likewise, $5 * 5 * 5 * 5$ becomes $5 \wedge 4$ or "five raised to the fourth power." QBasic allows you to raise a number to any positive real exponent, as in $12 \wedge 1.5$, or by any negative integer exponent, as in $19 \wedge -4$.

QBasic also includes two math operators that return integer values. Integer division, represented by a backslash (the opposite direction of the normal division operator), divides two values and returns the whole number of the result. For instance, in normal division when you divide 7 by 2, the result is 3.5. If you do an integer division, the result is 3 — the integer portion of the result.

The modulus (MOD) operator returns the integer remainder of a division. Using the same example, when you divide 7 by 2, the answer is 3 with a remainder of 1. Thus, the result of 7 MOD 2 is 1 (the remainder).

Comparison operators

Comparison operators are used to determine the relationship between two values. In other words, they are used to determine if one value is larger, smaller, or equal to another value. The result of using a comparison operator is always true (a value of −1) or false (a value of 0). Table 6-3 details the comparison operators available.

Table 6-3:   QBasic's Comparison Operators

Operator	Meaning
=	Equal
<	Less than
>	Greater than
<=	Less than or equal
>=	Greater than or equal
<>	Not equal

You will learn quite a bit about how to use comparison operators in Chapter 9.

String operators

In the previous section, you learned about QBasic's comparison operators. These same operators can also be used with strings to compare them with each other. When comparing strings, QBasic does its comparison from left to right, comparing each character with the corresponding character in the other string.

QBasic also allows you to use the plus (+) operator with strings. This operator is used to combine strings. In programming terminology, combining strings is referred to as *concatenation*. The following listing shows how concatenation works:

```
CLS
DIM FirstName AS STRING
DIM LastName AS STRING
DIM FullName AS STRING
FirstName = "Allen"
LastName = "Wyatt"
FullName = FirstName + " " + LastName
PRINT "My name is "; FullName
END
```

When this program is executed, the `FullName` variable contains the characters `Allen Wyatt`, as is printed on the screen. `FullName` is created by combining the contents of the `FirstName` variable (`Allen`) with a space (within the quote marks) and the contents of the `LastName` variable (`Wyatt`).

Logical operators

QBasic provides a number of operators you can use in logical formulas. These types of formulas are based on a branch of mathematics called Boolean logic. The logical operators are shown in Table 6-4.

Table 6-4:   QBasic's Logical Operators

Operator	Meaning
And	And
Eqv	Equivalent
Imp	Implication
Not	Not (or the logical opposite of)
Or	Or
Xor	Exclusive Or

Several of these operators are used in regular conversations on a daily basis. For instance, you may state "If I can get a raise and some time off, I will go on a vacation." This statement uses the logical AND. In this instance it means you will only go on a vacation if the first two conditions (raise and time off) are true. If either of them are not true (they are false), then you won't be going on a vacation.

You will learn more about some of the logical operators in Chapter 9. If you want to know more about Boolean logic, you may want to refer to a larger programming book that has more space for in-depth explanations.

CHAPTER 7
USING BUILT-IN FUNCTIONS

IN THIS CHAPTER

■ Converting strings

■ Manipulating strings

■ Creating strings

■ Using math functions

■ Using miscellaneous functions

One advantage of using a high-level programming language is that you can take advantage of any number of built-in functions it offers. The functions a language offers depend on the language itself and the version of the language. QBasic offers a large number of functions for manipulating dates, times, strings, and numbers. Built-in functions are important because they save you programming time and effort.

This chapter teaches you how to use QBasic's built-in functions in your programs. I cover the more useful and common functions here, and you can discover the others by using the built-in help system provided with QBasic.

String Functions

Historically, working with strings has always been a strong point of BASIC. QBasic is no exception — it includes many different functions you can use to create, manipulate, massage, and format strings.

Before I discuss strings, however, you'll find it helpful to understand how they are stored and used in a computer system. Computers store all their information (even strings) as numbers. Thus, characters are stored in a computer's memory using a numeric code. By representing a character with a number, the computer can work with a character the same way as it would any other number.

In order for computers to communicate with one another, a standard code is necessary for the representation of information. The first commonly used code for the exchange of computer information was ASCII (American Standard Code for Information Interchange). ASCII has codes only for the values 0 through 127. QBasic supports ASCII with an additional 128 characters. Thus, it supports character codes in the range of 0 through 255.

Changing the case of a string

To convert a string to all uppercase or all lowercase, you use the UCASE$ and LCASE$ functions. Use the string you want converted as an argument for one of these functions and the string is returned with the conversion complete.

To see how these functions work, enter the following program in QBasic:

```
MyString$ = "This Is a Mixed Case String"
CLS
PRINT "Original: "; MyString$
PRINT "Upper: "; UCASE$(MyString$)
PRINT "Lower: "; LCASE$(MyString$)
```

The output of the program is shown in Figure 7-1. Note that the program converts each character in the entire string, just as you requested.

Figure 7-1: You can quickly convert the case of a string.

Converting a string to a number

You'll want to convert a string to a number at times. This function comes in handy when you get input from a user in the form of a string, but you need to convert it to a number to process it further.

The VAL function converts the numbers in a string into a value. If the string contains any non-numeric characters, only the portion of the string before the first non-numeric character is converted. VAL will also properly convert a negative sign or exponentiation sign. Here's how you use the VAL function:

```
MyNumber = VAL(MyString$)
```

Converting a number to a string

The opposite of the VAL function is the STR$ function, which converts a number to a string. You may need to do this to format information for the screen or for your printer. The STR$ function correctly converts any number, including any negative sign. If the number being converted is positive, STR$ leaves a space at the beginning of the string for an implied plus sign.

The following code snippet shows how you use this function:

```
MyNumber = 3456
MyString$ = STR$(MyNumber)
```

When the code is executed, `MyString$` contains the characters `3456`. Notice the leading space, which is the placeholder for an implied plus sign.

Converting characters

Earlier in this chapter, you learned how computers use numbers to represent different characters internally. QBasic provides a function you can use to convert a character to the character code used to represent that character. The ASC function returns an integer value in the range of 0 through 255, depending on the character you use as an argument for the function.

The CHR$ function does just the opposite of the ASC function. CHR$ converts a numeric value (between 0 and 255) to its character equivalent. The following example shows how to use both the ASC and CHR$ functions:

```
MyString$ = "This is a string"
MyNum = 72
PRINT "Original string: "; MyString$
PRINT "Using ASC: "; ASC(MyString$)
PRINT "Original number: "; MyNum
PRINT "Using CHR$: "; CHR$(MyNum)
```

Finding the length of a string

The LEN function returns the length of a string, or the number of characters in the string. It is used quite often in programming. You use the function as follows:

```
Length = LEN(MyString$)
```

Note that the integer value LEN returns represents the total length of the string. This includes spaces and any other non-printing characters you cannot normally see in a string.

Extracting parts of a string

If you only need the leftmost or rightmost portions of a string, the LEFT$ and RIGHT$ functions are indispensable. All you need to do is tell QBasic how many characters to strip from the string.

For instance, in the following example, NewString$ contains the five leftmost characters of OldString$:

```
NewString$ = LEFT$(OldString$, 5)
```

This function does not change OldString$ at all; the characters are only copied. The following accomplishes the same task, instead pulling the five rightmost characters:

```
NewString$ = RIGHT$(OldString$, 5)
```

QBasic provides the MID$ function so you can pull characters from any given point in a string. This function is used extensively in programs.

To use the function, specify the name of the string, where you want to start pulling and (optionally) how many characters you want to pull. For instance, if you wanted to pull the fifth, sixth, and seventh characters from OldString$, you would use the following:

```
NewString$ = MID$(OldString$, 5, 3)
```

The third argument (3) specifies how many characters you want extracted, beginning with the character specified by the second argument (5). If you left off the third argument, then NewString$ would be equal to everything in OldString$ starting with the fifth character.

Finding strings within strings

Finding the location of one string within another is often helpful. The INSTR function (short for In String) allows you to quickly do this. You can use the function in two ways. You use the first form when you simply want to find the first occurrence of a string:

```
Place = INSTR(Big$, Small$)
```

When this code is finished, `Place` will contain a number representing where `Small$` was found within `Big$`. For instance, if `Big$` is equal to `My name is Allen` and `Small$` is equal to `name`, then `Place` will be equal to 4, since that is the character position where `name` begins in `Big$`. (Don't forget to count the space between `My` and `Name` as a character.)

You use the second form of INSTR if you want to begin searching from someplace other than the first character of the string. You use this version as follows:

```
Place = INSTR(5, Big$, Small$)
```

In this instance, the search starts with the fifth character of `Big$`. For instance, if `Big$` contained "This stuff is a really big string" and `Small$` contained "is", then you might be tempted to believe that INSTR would return a value of 3, where the first "is" occurs. However, INSTR actually returns a value of 12, which is the second occurrence, since you told it to start looking at character 5 in the string.

Math Functions

Mathematics is an integral part of our everyday lives. We do simple math many times each day. We figure out how long until we get off work, subtract items from our checking account, calculate the mileage our new car is getting, and perform a myriad of other tasks involving simple math.

Sometimes the math we need to do is a little more complex. If you're buying a house, you'll need more advanced functions to determine what your payments will be, given a particular interest rate, amount borrowed, and loan duration. If you are a scientist, engineer, or machinist or you have one of many occupations which require the use of more advanced functions, you'll appreciate the power inherent in QBasic's math functions. I cover many of these built-in math functions in the following sections.

Extracting an integer

If you're just interested in the portion of a number to the left of the decimal point, QBasic provides two different functions you can use. The INT function returns the next whole number lower than the original number, and the FIX function simply strips off the decimal portion of a number.

This distinction may not sound that great, but it can be when you are dealing with negative numbers. If the original number is –32.45, for instance, then INT would return –33 and FIX would return –32. The functions work as follows:

```
MyInt1 = INT(OrigNum)
MyInt2 = FIX(OrigNum)
```

Generating random numbers

If you've played games on a computer, you probably have seen the computer generate random numbers. Dealing cards, throwing dice, and other random occurrences are commonplace in some games. QBasic includes the RND function so you can generate your own random numbers.

The RND function returns a single-precision number greater than 0 and less than 1. Before using the function for the first time, most programmers use the RANDOMIZE statement. This forces QBasic to shake things up a bit by *reseeding* its random-number generator — sort of like shaking the dice or shuffling the cards. You should include the following at the beginning of any program in which you use random numbers:

```
RANDOMIZE TIMER
```

This forces QBasic to reseed the random-number generator using the value stored in the internal timer used by your computer. (It can't get much more random than that.)

Determining the sign of a number

When you perform a mathematical operation, you sometimes need to know the sign of a number or whether the number is equal to zero. The SGN function is used to determine the sign of a number. You use the function as follows:

```
NumSign = SGN(MyNumber)
```

When this code has executed, NumSign will be equal to one of three values. If NumSign is equal to –1, then MyNumber is negative. If NumSign is equal to zero, then so is MyNumber. If NumSign is equal to 1, then MyNumber is positive.

Finding an absolute

You probably remember from your math classes that the absolute value of a number is its positive equivalent. Thus, the absolute value of both –3 and 3 is 3. QBasic provides the ABS function to return the absolute value of a number. You use the function as follows:

```
NumAbsolute = ABS(OrigNum)
```

Miscellaneous Functions

QBasic includes several additional functions that don't fit into any of the categories discussed so far. These functions have to do with determining the date and time and with making irritating noises.

Determining the date

The DATE$ function is the starting point for many calculations involving dates. The function returns the date programmed into your computer in the format MM-DD-YYYY. To see how this function works, enter this program:

```
DIM Today AS STRING
DIM Month AS INTEGER
DIM Day AS INTEGER
DIM Year AS INTEGER
Today = DATE$
Month = VAL(LEFT$(Today, 2))
Day = VAL(MID$(Today, 4, 2))
Year = VAL(RIGHT$(Today, 4))
CLS
PRINT "Today is "; Today
PRINT
PRINT "Month:"; Month
PRINT "Day:"; Day
PRINT "Year:"; Year
```

Note that the example uses several different string manipulation functions to pull Today apart and convert its different constituents into numbers. The LEFT$ function strips away the first two characters from the left of the string (Today) created by the DATE$ function to get the month, the MID$ function grabs the fourth and fifth characters from the Today string to get the day, and the RIGHT$ function strips away the last four characters of the Today string to get the year. (The date lines in Figure 7-2 show you the results of this program.) When you use the VAL function to extract the values, you are converting the text characters in the `Today` string to their numeric equivalents. `Month`, `Day`, and `Year` are numeric variables, so they don't print any leading zeros that might have been in the original `Today` string. (If the month in the string was `08`, it prints out as 8 when converted to a numeric value by the `VAL` function.)

Determining the time

Not only does your computer keep internal track of the date, it also keeps track of the time of day. You can retrieve this information by using the TIME$ function. The function returns a string representing the current time in the format HH:MM:SS. The following example program is an extension of the program used in the previous section. It shows how to use the TIME$ function.

```
DIM Today AS STRING
DIM Now AS STRING
DIM Month AS INTEGER
DIM Day AS INTEGER
DIM Year AS INTEGER
DIM Hour AS INTEGER
DIM Minute AS INTEGER
DIM Second AS INTEGER
Today = DATE$
Now = TIME$
Month = VAL(LEFT$(Today, 2))
Day = VAL(MID$(Today, 4, 2))
Year = VAL(RIGHT$(Today, 4))
Hour = VAL(LEFT$(Now, 2))
Minute = VAL(MID$(Now, 4, 2))
Second = VAL(RIGHT$(Now, 2))
CLS
PRINT "Today is "; Today
PRINT "It is currently "; Now
PRINT
PRINT "Month:"; Month
PRINT "Day:"; Day
```

```
PRINT "Year:"; Year
PRINT
PRINT "Hour:"; Hour
PRINT "Minute"; Minute
PRINT "Second:"; Second
```

When you run the program, the output appears similar to what is shown in Figure 7-2.

Figure 7-2: QBasic can return information concerning the date and time.

Making noise

If you want, you can cause your PC to make an annoying beep. You do this, oddly enough, with the BEEP statement. This type of sound is typically used to signal some error condition or to alert the user that some intervention is necessary. All you need to do to sound the speaker is use the BEEP statement on its own program line:

```
BEEP
```

CHAPTER 8
DEVELOPING PROCEDURES

IN THIS CHAPTER

- Understanding procedures
- Creating subroutines
- Creating functions
- Procedures and variables

You learned about modular programming in Chapter 2. This approach allows you to break programs down into smaller, easier-to-handle modules.

This chapter teaches you how to implement the modular approach to programming using QBasic. When you are done with this chapter, you'll understand how to make your program as modular as possible.

What are Procedures?

In QBasic, a *procedure* is another name for a program module. Procedures are a way for you to chop up your program into small building blocks that you can use any way you want.

Procedures have not always been available in programming languages. In fact, their use is not mandatory in QBasic. After you understand the rationale behind them, however, you can see why they're beneficial and how to best use them.

The need for procedures

As your programs get larger, you'll start to notice something very interesting — your programming code starts to repeat itself. For instance, you may want to print information on the computer screen so it is centered from left to right. The programming code to easily do this is as follows:

```
A$ = "Center This"
X% = (80 - LEN(A$))\2
PRINT TAB(X%); A$
```

This code determines the length of what you want to center (A$) using the LEN function. It then subtracts that value from the screen width (80 characters) and divides the result by 2. The PRINT statement then starts printing at that location on the line, using the built-in TAB function.

This code works great, provided you have only one thing you need to center. Imagine, however, that you have five lines you need to center on the screen. In that case, your program could easily start looking like this:

```
A$ = "Discovery Computing Inc."
X% = (80 - LEN(A$))\2
PRINT TAB(X%); A$
A$ = "PO Box 11356"
X% = (80 - LEN(A$))\2
PRINT TAB(X%); A$
A$ = "Cincinnati, OH 45211"
X% = (80 - LEN(A$))\2
PRINT TAB(X%); A$
A$ = "voice: 513-598-4300"
X% = (80 - LEN(A$))\2
PRINT TAB(X%); A$
A$ = "www.dcomp.com"
X% = (80 - LEN(A$))\2
PRINT TAB(X%); A$
```

Do you see the repetition? At this point, your code can quickly get out of hand, particularly if you need to make a change to where the five lines are printed on the screen — for instance, if your boss wants you to move all five lines five spaces to the left.

How procedures work

Procedures work by allowing you to gather repetitive code into a single module that can be called over and over again. For instance, in the previous example, you may want to create a procedure that does the actual centering of the text on the screen. This concept is shown in Figure 8-1.

Figure 8-1:   Procedures are handled outside the normal linear program flow.

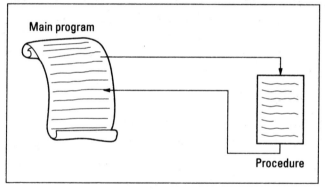

Main program

Procedure

When a procedure is called up from the main program — for instance, when you need to center some text — the program begins executing the code in the procedure instead of the code in the main program. When the procedure is done, program execution returns to the main program at the point immediately after the procedure was first called up.

What should be in a procedure?

You already know that repetitive code is a good candidate for a procedure. However, many programmers tend to use procedures even though the procedure may only be called up once in their program.

The reason for this is quite simple — procedures can be used as an organizational tool in your program. Putting a programming task into a procedure instead of in the main program allows you to more easily organize what your program needs to do.

Procedures in QBasic

Different programming languages use procedures in different ways. In QBasic, you can create two types of procedures: subroutines and functions. In reality, these two types of procedures are very similar. The only major difference between the two of these is that functions return a value to the calling program, whereas subroutines do not. In the balance of this chapter you learn how to use both subroutines and functions.

Creating Subroutines

You can create subroutines in QBasic in two ways. The first is to use the menu system and choose Edit⇨New Sub. When you do, QBasic asks you for a subroutine name, as shown in Figure 8-2.

Figure 8-2: You must provide a name for a new subroutine.

After you provide a name and click OK, you are ready to start entering the programming code for the subroutine.

The easier way to create a subroutine, however, is to enter the SUB keyword, followed by the name of the subroutine, and press Enter.

Regardless of the method you use to create your subroutine, QBasic displays it by itself in the Program window after you start to work on it. Your main program is still there; it's just hidden from view so you can work on the subroutine.

As an example of how to create a subroutine, suppose you wanted a subroutine that cleared the screen and placed a header at the center of the top line. When the subroutine is complete, the screen would be ready to receive additional information. You decide to name this subroutine NewPage.

In order to create such a subroutine, enter the following line in the Program window:

```
SUB NewPage
```

When you press Enter at the end of the line, QBasic creates a new subroutine for you and leaves your screen looking like Figure 8-3.

Figure 8-3:   Your subroutine is started and ready to be programmed.

Notice that when QBasic creates a new subroutine, the boundaries of the subroutine are denoted by two lines of code. The subroutine starts with the SUB keyword and ends with the END SUB line. Everything you enter between these two lines is part of the subroutine.

Now, type the program lines you want in the subroutine. In this case, type these lines:

```
CLS
A$ = "Discovery Computing Inc."
X% = (80 - LEN(A$))\2
PRINT TAB(X%); A$
PRINT
```

These lines instruct QBasic to clear the screen, center a company name on the first line, and then print a blank line.

Using your subroutine

To use the subroutine, you need to switch back to your main program. You do this by choosing View⇨SUBs. This displays a list of procedures in your program, as shown in Figure 8-4.

Figure 8-4:   QBasic keeps track of the procedures in your program.

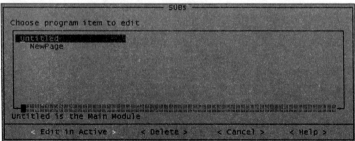

Notice that two program items are shown in Figure 8-4. The top one (Untitled, in this case) is the main program you are developing. If you were working on a previously saved program, that name would be shown instead of Untitled. The second item in the list is the single subroutine you have defined for your program. If there were additional procedures, they would be listed, as well.

Note, also, that the NewPage subroutine name is indented. This indicates that it belongs to the main program (Untitled). To start working on the main program again, choose the top item in the list and click the Edit in Active option. Your main program again appears in the Program window.

In order to use your new subroutine, you need to instruct QBasic to call it up. You do this simply by using the name of the subroutine on a program line by itself. Type the following into the Program window as your main program:

```
NewPage
PRINT "QBasic is now back from the subroutine and
running the main program."
PRINT
PRINT "There are many ways you can use
subroutines in your programs."
```

When you run the program, QBasic treats the NewPage command (on the first line) as if it were a keyword. It locates the subroutine of the same name and then executes that subroutine. When the subroutine is completed (the END SUB line is reached), the main program resumes at the very next line. The resulting output is shown in Figure 8-5.

Using subroutine arguments

QBasic also allows you to specify values to be used by your subroutine. This capability can make your subroutines very powerful, indeed. For instance, you may want to modify your NewPage subroutine so that you can use it with any page title you want. In order to do this, you need to switch back to viewing the NewPage subroutine in the Program window and then modify the SUB NewPage program line so it reflects what you are planning to pass to the subroutine.

Figure 8-5: Subroutines can be used to produce output.

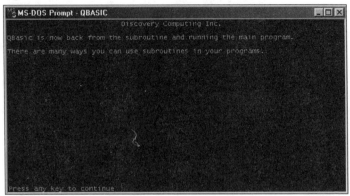

You want to pass a title, which is a string, to the subroutine. Change the subroutine so it appears as follows:

```
SUB NewPage (A$)
CLS
X% = (80 - LEN(A$))\2
PRINT TAB(X%); A$
PRINT
END SUB
```

Notice that A$ now appears in parentheses on the subroutine declaration line. This informs QBasic that NewPage uses a string value and that string will be passed to the subroutine. Notice that the line assigning a value to A$ has been removed from the subroutine. It is no longer needed; the string is supplied by the program invoking the subroutine.

To use the subroutine, you slightly modify the way in which it is called up. Notice from the following how the first line has been changed from what I presented earlier in the chapter.

```
NewPage "John's Bagel Shop"
PRINT "QBasic is now back from the subroutine and
running the main program."
PRINT
```

```
PRINT "There are many ways you can use
subroutines in your programs."
```

All that has been changed is that the string the subroutine will use has been added directly after the subroutine name. When you run the program, the new title appears on the screen, as expected.

Creating Functions

You create functions in QBasic by choosing Edit➪New Function. QBasic prompts you for the name of the function you want to use, as shown in Figure 8-6.

Figure 8-6:   You must provide a name for your new function.

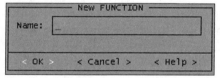

When you enter a function name and choose OK, QBasic creates the function and allows you to begin programming it.

For example, say you wanted to create a function that would convert Fahrenheit temperatures into their equivalent on the Kelvin scale. Obviously, you need to pass your function a temperature (the initial Fahrenheit temperature), convert it, and pass back the calculated temperature.

To work with this example, start a brand-new program and enter the following function:

```
FUNCTION Kelvin! (Degrees AS SINGLE)
  Kelvin! = (Degrees + 459.67) / 1.8
END FUNCTION
```

Quite a few similarities exist between how a function like this is put together and the way in which subroutines are constructed. Notice that you can pass arguments, just as you do with subroutines, and that the function is terminated with the END keyword (END FUNCTION in this case, as opposed to END SUB in subroutines).

There are some important differences, however, between subroutines and functions. First, note that the function name has a data type suffix on it. (I discuss data type suffixes in Chapter 6.) The suffix tells QBasic what type of data your function will return to the calling program. In this case, the exclamation point informs QBasic that the function returns a single-precision number.

The body of the function, in this case, is quite short. It uses the Degrees argument to calculate the temperature on the Kelvin scale. The value is assigned to the variable Kelvin!. This is extremely important; it is the same as the name of the function. Without this notation, QBasic would not know what to return to the calling program.

To see how the Kelvin function works, enter the following main program:

```
CLS
INPUT "Degrees Fahrenheit? ", A!
PRINT
PRINT A!; "degrees Fahrenheit is the same as";
PRINT Kelvin(A!);
PRINT "degrees on the Kelvin scale."
```

When you run the program, the first line clears the screen. The second line prompts you to enter a temperature on the Fahrenheit scale. The value you type is assigned to the variable A! as soon as you press Enter. This value is then used in the fourth and fifth lines. In the fourth line it is printed just as you entered it. In the fifth line, it is passed to the Kelvin function, whose result is printed on the screen. The output from the program is shown in Figure 8-7.

Figure 8-7: The results of functions can be printed.

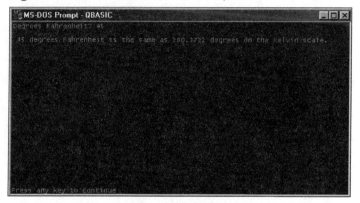

Procedures and Variables

So far in this chapter you have used quite a few variables in your procedures. Variables you use in procedures are treated a bit differently than you might think, however. You already know that if you use a variable in your program, you can assign different values to that variable. When a new value is assigned to the variable, the old value is discarded. If you use a variable in a procedure and that variable is the same as one in your main program (or in a different procedure), the values of each of these variables are kept separate from each other. This feature allows you to reuse your subroutines from one program to another without much concern about unwanted results due to the variables used in the procedures being shared.

This ability to compartmentalize variables is known in programming terms as *scope*. The *scope* of a variable means the area of your program in which it is valid. By default, variables in a procedure only have scope for the procedure in which they are defined. To see how this works, enter the following subroutine in a brand-new program:

```
SUB CheckVar
  X = 3 * 5.9723
  PRINT "A. CheckVar's value for X is now"; X
  PRINT
  X = X / .439
  PRINT "B. CheckVar's value for X is now"; X
  PRINT
END SUB
```

This subroutine first calculates the value of X (17.9169) and displays it. Then it modifies X by dividing it by .439 (resulting in a value of 40.8128) and displays the value again.

Now, enter the following as the main program that utilizes the CheckVar subroutine:

```
CLS
X = 1234
PRINT "1. Main program value of X is"; X
PRINT
X = X ^ .5
PRINT "2. Calling procedure; value of X is"; X
PRINT
CheckVar
PRINT "3. Back from procedure; value of X is"; X
PRINT
X = X * 15.32
PRINT "4. Main program value of X is"; X
```

In this example, program X is first set equal to a value of 1234. It is then raised to a power of .5 (one-half), which is the same as the square root of X, or a value of 35.1283. The CheckVar subroutine is then called, and finally, the value in X is multiplied by 15.32, resulting in a value of 538.1661.

When you run the program, note that at Steps 2 and 3 (as shown in Figure 8-8), the value of X is the same. This means that the value of X was not changed while the subroutine was running.

Another important consideration concerning variables in procedures is that their values are reinitialized whenever you start the procedure again. Thus, if you call up a procedure five times in your program, the variables in the procedure are created in each instance, and the values are discarded upon ending the procedure.

In most cases, this type of behavior is desirable. In some instances, however, you may want to maintain the value of variables within a procedure without having them discarded. (The structure and purpose of your procedure will dictate whether you want to maintain variable values.) To retain the values of procedure variables from one instance to another, you use the STATIC keyword. To see how this works, add the following subroutine to your program:

```
SUB KeepIt STATIC
 X = X + 1
 PRINT " - Value of X in KeepIt is"; X
 PRINT
END SUB
```

Note that you add the STATIC keyword to the end of the first line in the subroutine — the same one that contains the SUB keyword. Now you can add the following lines to the end of your main program:

```
PRINT
KeepIt
KeepIt
KeepIt
PRINT "5. Main program value of X is"; X
```

These program lines result in calling the KeepIt subroutine three times. The output of the program is shown in Figure 8-8. Note that the value of X is maintained for the KeepIt procedure. If the STATIC keyword were removed from the subroutine, then each instance in which KeepIt was used would display that the value of the variable was 1.

Figure 8-8: The STATIC keyword instructs QBasic to protect the values of variables in a procedure.

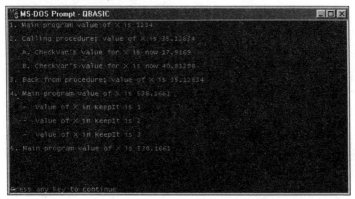

CHAPTER 9
UNDERSTANDING PROGRAMMING STRUCTURES

IN THIS CHAPTER

- For . . . Next loops
- While . . . Wend structures
- Do Loop structures
- If . . . Then structures
- Select Case structures

So far in this book, you've focused on performing well-defined sequential tasks using QBasic. These tasks are instructive, but they're not indicative of the real power in computers — the ability to make decisions and repetitively perform operations. This chapter introduces you to the powerful world of programming structures.

Using a For . . . Next Loop

One of the most common programming structures you will use is known as the For . . . Next loop. This structure allows you to execute a set of instructions a specific number of times.

The format of the For . . . Next loop is illustrated by the following program code:

```
FOR J = 1 TO 10
  PRINT J
NEXT J
```

In a For . . . Next loop such as this, everything between the FOR line and the NEXT line is executed however many times you indicate on the FOR line. (The lines in the loop are indented here for clarity.) In this case, the intervening instructions are executed ten times. Each time through the loop, the value of the counter used after the FOR statement (in this case, the variable J) is incremented by one. Thus, if you run the above code, the numbers 1 through 10 are printed, indicating the value of J on each iteration through the loop.

One of the most common uses of For . . . Next loops is to step through arrays. (You learned about variable arrays in Chapter 6.) For example, type the following program in your computer (I use Dow to stand for Day of the Week):

```
DIM Dow(7) AS STRING
DIM Day AS INTEGER
Dow(1) = "Sunday"
Dow(2) = "Monday"
Dow(3) = "Tuesday"
Dow(4) = "Wednesday"
Dow(5) = "Thursday"
Dow(6) = "Friday"
Dow(7) = "Saturday"
CLS
FOR Day = 1 TO 7
  PRINT Day, Dow(Day)
NEXT Day
```

When you run the program, the output looks like Figure 9-1. Using the For . . . Next loop to process the array is much easier and more versatile than using individual PRINT statements to display each member of the array. The beauty of For . . . Next loops is that you're able to process quite a bit of data with just a couple of program lines.

Using different loop values

You are not limited to using sequential loop values beginning with 1 (although this is the most common method of using loops). Indeed, you can use any numbers in the loop you want. For instance, the following is a valid loop:

```
FOR J = 27 TO 43
  PRINT J
NEXT J
```

Figure 9-1:   Loops allow you to quickly process data using fewer program lines.

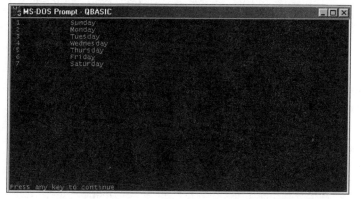

In this case, the variable J (the loop counter) will range in value from 27 to 43 on each successive iteration. You can even use variables to indicate the beginning and ending values of the range to use in the loop.

Exiting a For . . . Next loop

Normally, a For . . . Next loop progresses until the counter is either greater than the upper range (if stepping in a positive direction) or lower than the lower range (if stepping negatively).

If you need to exit a For . . . Next loop before it would normally finish, use the EXIT FOR statement. As an example, consider the following short program:

```
DIM Where AS INTEGER
DIM J AS INTEGER
CLS
INPUT "Exit point?", Where
PRINT
FOR J = 1 TO 50
  PRINT "Got to"; J
  IF J = Where THEN EXIT FOR
NEXT J
```

This example program uses an IF statement, which you learn about later in this chapter. If you run the program, you see that if you enter a value between 1 and 50, the program exits the loop early. If you enter a value outside that range, then the For . . . Next loop finishes as normal. The PRINT statement within the For. . .Next loop is used to notify you of the current iteration of the loop. (You will see this right away if you run the program.)

Using a While . . . Wend Structure

If you must perform an action over and over until some condition is met, but you don't know how many times it must be done beforehand, you can use a While . . . Wend loop. This loop checks whatever condition you specify. If the condition is true, then the code within the loop (between the WHILE and WEND keywords) is executed. If it is not true, then the code is not executed. The following is an example:

```
MyNum = 0
WHILE MyNum < 1 OR MyNum > 10
  INPUT "Pick a number between 1 and 10:", MyNum
WEND
```

This small code snippet will continue to ask the user for a number until one is entered that is between 1 and 10. Note that there must be some code within the While . . . Wend loop that forces the condition to become false. If there is not, then the loop will never end.

QBasic's Do Loop Structures

One of QBasic's most versatile and capable looping constructs is the Do loop. Two versions of the structure exist. One is referred to as the Do While loop, and the other is the Do Until loop. The Do While loop allows you to check a condition and then execute a block of code if that condition is met. If the condition isn't met, the block of code is skipped over.

To see how a Do While loop works, enter the following:

```
DIM OrigNum AS INTEGER
DIM CountNum AS INTEGER
DIM CalcNum AS LONG
CLS
INPUT "What number"; OrigNum
CountNum = OrigNum
DO WHILE CountNum > 0
CalcNum = CalcNum * CountNum
CountNum = CountNum - 1
LOOP
PRINT "The factorial of"; OrigNum;
PRINT "is"; CalcNum
```

When you run the program and enter a number, the Do While loop is used to calculate the factorial of the number. A factorial is derived by multiplying all the numbers less than or equal to the number whose factorial you want. For instance, if you want the factorial of 5, you would multiply $5 \times 4 \times 3 \times 2 \times 1$, resulting in 120. Likewise, the factorial of 6 is 720.

In this case, the variable CountNum is used to control the Do While loop and the CalcNum variable is used to store the cumulative value of the factorial itself. Note that the value of CountNum is modified in the body of the loop. If you were looking for the factorial of 12 (OrigNum is 12), then CountNum would start out at 12. Each pass through the loop results in `CountNum` being decremented by one. The loop is repeated as long as `CountNum` is greater than zero. When it is equal to zero, then the loop test proves false and the loop is exited. (Remember that the loop is only executed as long as the condition is true. When the condition becomes false, the loop is completed.)

By using the Do Until version of the loop, you check the condition at the end of the block of code. The block of code is thus always executed at least once. This can come in handy for some purposes, such as getting input from the user. The following version of the factorial program uses two loops, one inside the other — a Do Until loop was placed "around" the entire body of the program.

```
DIM OrigNum AS INTEGER
DIM CountNum AS INTEGER
DIM CalcNum AS LONG
CLS
DO
INPUT "What number (0 to exit)"; OrigNum
CountNum = OrigNum
CalcNum = 0
DO WHILE CountNum > 0
  CalcNum = CalcNum * CountNum
  CountNum = CountNum - 1
LOOP
PRINT "The factorial of"; OrigNum;
PRINT "is"; CalcNum
PRINT
LOOP UNTIL OrigNum = 0
END
```

As written here, the outer Do Until version of the loop checks to see if the number the user entered was 0. If it was, then the program is exited. If it was not, then the loop is repeated and the user can enter another number. Figure 9-2 shows an example session with this program.

This program example presents an important concept — you can nest loops inside one another. Nesting, if used properly, offers some powerful programming methods that you can use to accomplish tasks.

You exit a Do loop early by using the EXIT DO keyword. This works the same way as the EXIT FOR keyword worked in a For . . . Next loop. When QBasic encounters it, it jumps out of the currently executing Do loop and continues processing as if the loop had ended normally.

Figure 9-2:   Loops can be used to repeatedly request user input.

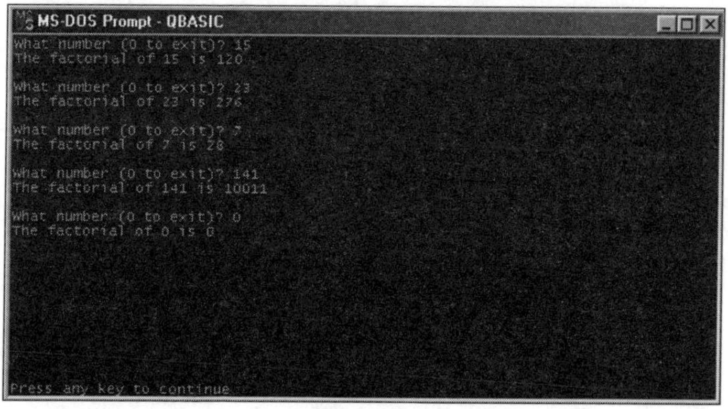

```
MS-DOS Prompt - QBASIC
What number (0 to exit)? 15
The factorial of 15 is 120

What number (0 to exit)? 23
The factorial of 23 is 276

What number (0 to exit)? 7
The factorial of 7 is 28

What number (0 to exit)? 141
The factorial of 141 is 10011

What number (0 to exit)? 0
The factorial of 0 is 0




Press any key to continue
```

Using an If . . . Then Structure

The If . . . Then structure is perhaps the most used of any programming structure. This fact is not surprising, as it directly reflects how humans think. We use the same sort of structures in making our daily decisions. For instance, you may tell a friend, "If you drive, then we can go to the show." Likewise, your boss may say, "If Ms. Spackleford calls before 3:00, then put her right through to me. If she doesn't call, then try to contact her at her office."

Both of these are everyday examples of what QBasic refers to as an If . . . Then structure. Though the everyday examples may be formed a bit different than they would be in QBasic, the purpose is exactly the same. If these statements were to be formed as required by QBasic, they would look similar to this:

```
IF you drive THEN
we can go to the show
END IF
IF Ms. Spackleford calls THEN
put her right through to me
ELSE
call her at her office
END IF
```

At first, this structure may look a bit funny, but hopefully you can see the striking parallels between your normal conversation and what QBasic uses. QBasic recognizes two different formats for an If . . . Then structure. The first is a single-line version, as follows:

```
IF condition THEN action
```

All you need to do is supply the condition and the action, of course. Earlier in this chapter, I used a single-line If . . . Then structure when I discussed the EXIT FOR keyword:

```
FOR J = 1 TO 50
  PRINT "Got to "; J
  IF J = Where THEN EXIT FOR
NEXT J
```

In this case, the For . . . Next loop was exited early (using EXIT FOR) if the specified condition was met. Many of your If . . . Then structures will fit into this single-line mold. For more complex structures, you can break the If . . . Then structure up over several lines, as follows:

```
IF condition THEN
[do this stuff]
ELSEIF condition THEN
[do this stuff]
```

```
ELSE
[do this stuff]
END IF
```

Lots of stuff is going on in this structure! Each major portion of the structure defines a block of code that will be executed if the specified conditions are met. The first block is executed if the original IF condition is met. In that case, the rest of the structure is ignored. If that condition is not met, then QBasic checks out the ELSEIF condition. If it is met, then that block is executed and the rest of the structure is ignored. Finally, if the ELSEIF condition is not met, then the ELSE block is executed and the structure is complete.

You should note that the ELSEIF and ELSE blocks are completely optional. You can use them if your logic dictates they be used, but you don't have to.

If . . . Then structures are used very frequently in programming. One of the most common uses is to check if values are within acceptable limits or if the user followed instructions. The following program illustrates this concept:

```
DIM Months(12) AS STRING
DIM NameWanted AS STRING
DIM Mon AS INTEGER
DIM Found AS INTEGER
DIM MonPos AS STRING
Months(1) = "January"
Months(2) = "February"
Months(3) = "March"
Months(4) = "April"
Months(5) = "May"
Months(6) = "June"
Months(7) = "July"
Months(8) = "August"
Months(9) = "September"
Months(10) = "October"
Months(11) = "November"
```

```
Months(12) = "December"
CLS
INPUT "Month Name? ", NameWanted
Found = 0
FOR Mon = 1 TO 12
  IF Months(Mon) = NameWanted THEN Found = Mon
NEXT Mon
IF Found = 1 THEN MonPos = "1st"
IF Found = 2 THEN MonPos = "2nd"
IF Found = 3 THEN MonPos = "3rd"
IF Found > 3 THEN
MonPos = MID$(STR$(Found), 2)
MonPos = MonPos + "th"
END IF
PRINT
IF Found > 0 THEN
PRINT "The month '"; NameWanted;
PRINT "' is the "; MonPos; " month."
ELSE
PRINT NameWanted; " could not be found."
END IF
```

This program uses both versions of the If . . . Then structure. In fact, five individual If . . . Then structures are in the program. They are used extensively to put together the MonPos string, and one is used to create the final printed output. For example, the fourth If . . . Then structure checks to see if Found is greater than 3. If it is, then MonPos is set equal to the string equivalent of Found. As an example, if Found is equal to 6, then the STR$ function returns a value of 6, with a leading space. The MID$ function is then used to return just the portion of that string starting with the second character, or the part right after the space. Finally, that string (6) is assigned to MonPos, and the next line adds the characters th to the string.

Earlier in the chapter, you learned how to nest loops. You can also nest If . . . Then structures in your program.

Using the Select Case Structure

As you program more and more, you will discover that the solutions to many programming problems require long and often complicated If . . . Then structures or a long series of the structures. For instance, in the last section a series of If . . . Then structures were used, as follows:

```
IF Found = 1 THEN MonPos = "1st"
IF Found = 2 THEN MonPos = "2nd"
IF Found = 3 THEN MonPos = "3rd"
IF Found > 3 THEN
MonPos = MID$(STR$(Found), 2)
MonPos = MonPos + "th"
END IF
```

In instances such as this, the use of If . . . Then structures can become a bit cumbersome. You can use QBasic's Select Case structure, which can rid your programs of the long processions of If . . . Then structures. If the foregoing code was rewritten to use a Select Case structure, it would appear as follows:

```
SELECT CASE Found
CASE 1
  MonPos = "1st"
CASE 2
  MonPos = "2nd"
CASE 3
  MonPos = "3rd"
CASE ELSE
  MonPos = MID$(STR$(Found), 2)
  MonPos = MonPos + "th"
END SELECT
```

This may appear a bit longer, but it is much more understandable than the series of If . . . Then structures previously used. In this case, the SELECT CASE statement indicates what is to be tested in the structure. Here, the variable being tested is Found. Each instance of the CASE keyword within the structure indicates another test being performed. The first test is whether Found is equal to 1. If it is, then the block of program code under that CASE statement is executed. If not, then the next test is performed. Finally, if none of the tests succeeds, the block of code after the CASE ELSE statement is executed.

You can have as many CASE tests within the struture as you desire, and the CASE ELSE statement is optional. QBasic provides a variety of ways you can put together a CASE test. The test can be:

■ An explicit value such as 3 or "M".

■ A numeric or string expression such as Val(MyString) or ThisString$.

■ A range of values by using the TO keyword, as in "A" TO "Z" or 5 TO 9.

■ A conditional range of values by using the IS keyword, as in IS.

CLIFFSNOTES REVIEW

Use this CliffsNotes Review to practice what you've learned in this book and to build your confidence in doing the job right the first time. After you work through the review questions, the problem-solving exercises, and the fun and useful practice projects, you're well on your way to achieving your goal of writing your first computer program.

Q&A

1. Which of the following is an example of a low-level computer language?

a. BASIC

b. C/C++

c. Assembly language

d. Pascal

2. Which of the following versions of BASIC could you use if you needed to develop a program for the Macintosh?

a. True BASIC

b. Visual Basic

c. QBasic

d. Standard BASIC

3. Which of the following variable types is used to store textual information?

a. integer

b. string

c. long

d. double

4. What does the RIGHT$ function do?

   a. Right-justifies your program lines.

   b. Corrects any errors detected in your program.

   c. Allows you to extract information from the middle of a string.

   d. Returns a specified number of characters from the right end of a string.

   Answers: (1) c. (2) a. (3) b. (4) d.

Scenarios

1. You are being hired as a programming consultant for a small business in your community. Name the three primary factors you would consider in choosing the programming language to use for your project.

2. You are faced with writing a portion of a computer program in BASIC that will display the contents of a string array that contains 25 elements. Write the program lines to do this using a For . . . Next loop. Make sure the display also shows the element number (1, 2, 3, . . . 24, 25) that is being displayed.

   Answers: (1) Which language, if any, is already in use at the company; what computer configuration (hardware, operating system, etc.) the program will run on; and what language best meets the needs of the program being designed. (2). Possible code is

```
FOR X = 1 TO 25
  PRINT X, MyArray$(X)
NEXT X
```

Visual Test

Use the following program code to answer the questions that follow:

```
FUNCTION MyFunc$ (Orig AS STRING)
 DIM Olen AS INTEGER
 DIM J AS INTEGER
 DIM NStr AS STRING
 NStr = ""
 Olen = LEN(Orig)
 FOR J = 1 TO Olen
  NStr = MID$(Orig, J, 1) + NStr
 NEXT J
 MyFunc$ = NStr
 END FUNCTION
```

1. What type of procedure is this? How do you know?

2. What type of argument is passed to the procedure? What is the name of the argument, as used in the procedure?

3. Does the procedure return a value? What type of value does it return?

4. What is the purpose of the procedure?

Answers: (1) It is a function. You can tell because it uses the FUNCTION keyword to declare the procedure. (2) A string is passed to the procedure. The argument's name is Orig. (3) The procedure returns a string value. (4) It reverses a string that is passed to it.

Practice Projects

1. Using QBasic, write a procedure that returns a random integer value between 1 and 50.

2. Using QBasic, write a program that uses the procedure you developed in Exercise 1. The program should clear the screen, call the procedure 20 times, and display a horizontal bar chart that indicates (using asterisks) the results of each call of the procedure.

Answers: (1) Possible code is

```
FUNCTION RanNum%
  RanNum% = INT(50 * RND + 1)
END FUNCTION
```

(2) Possible code is

```
DIM J AS INTEGER
DIM NewNum AS INTEGER
RANDOMIZE TIMER
CLS
FOR J = 1 TO 20
  NewNum = RanNum%
  PRINT STRING$(NewNum, "*")
NEXT J
```

CLIFFSNOTES RESOURCE CENTER

Obviously, CliffsNotes *Writing Your First Computer Program* can only begin to scratch the surface of computer programming. You have already created your first program, and you may be ready to venture further into the deep end of the programming pool.

With this desire in mind, I have put together this CliffsNotes Resource Center to provide links to the best information in print and online about computer programming.

Books

This CliffsNotes book is one of many great books about computer programming published by IDG Books Worldwide, Inc. So if you want some great books to continue your exploration of computer programming, check out some of these IDG Books Worldwide publications, as well as some titles by other publishers:

Visual Basic 6 For Dummies. Ready to step up from QBasic? Wally Wang offers a great introduction to Microsoft's popular Visual Basic programming environment for Windows. IDG Books Worldwide, $29.99.

C For Dummies. Actually a two-volume set to programming in C, Dan Gookin lets you move at your own speed as you learn about the C language. IDG Books Worldwide, $39.99.

C++ For Dummies. Read this book *after* you already know how to program in C. Stephen Davis guides you through the extensions that make C++ what it is. IDG Books Worldwide, $29.99.

Visual C++ 6 For Dummies Quick Reference. Don't pay too much attention to the title of this book. Charles Wright provides more than just a quick reference to the Visual C++ implementation of the language. This is a great introduction to the topic, and it's also a good book for novices. IDG Books Worldwide, $14.99.

COBOL For Dummies. Arthur Griffith offers a good introductory-level treatment of the most popular programming language in the world. Includes a CD-ROM with great development tools. IDG Books Worldwide, $29.99.

Just Java 2. Peter van der Linden focuses on teaching Java to absolute beginners using the most valuable parts of the language. Can't go wrong with this one. Prentice Hall, $44.99.

Learn Pascal in Three Days. This book for beginners takes a learn-by-example approach. Sam Abolrous focuses on the structured aspects of the language as a foundation for professional programming. Wordware Publishing, $24.95.

It's easy to find books published by IDG Books Worldwide, Inc. You'll find them in your favorite bookstores (on the Internet and at a store near you). We also have three web sites that you can use to read about all the books we publish:

■ www.cliffsnotes.com

■ www.dummies.com

■ www.idgbooks.com

Internet

Check out these Web sites for more information on computer programming:

BASIC Programming Gurus, www.basicguru.com/, acts as an online resource for you to get help with your BASIC programming efforts. A series of experts are available to help, regardless of your needs.

Carl & Gary's Visual Basic Home Page, www.cgvb.com/, is one of the best resource sites on the Web for Visual Basic programming. Great set of archives and online code.

Coder's Knowledge Base, www.netalive.org/ckb/, provides resources and online code for those using Pascal and Delphi. You can also subscribe to an e-mail newsletter here.

JavaWorld, www.javaworld.com/, offers a little bit of everything related to Java. Run like an online magazine, with articles, departments, tips, and advertisements.

Visual C++ Resources, www.aul.fiu.edu/tech/visualc.html, provides a wide assortment of resources available to the Visual C++ programmer. Includes a large number of links to newsgroups and FAQs.

Magazines & Other Media

Most magazines devoted to programming mix information for the beginner and the veteran. In addition, many offer trial subscriptions. Even though the suggestions here are for print magazines, I have included Web page information so you can check them out.

Access-Office-VB Advisor, www.advisor.com/av.html, focuses on various forms of Visual Basic, particularly VBA (for Microsoft applications). Helpful information for all levels of programmers.

C/C++ Users Journal, www.cuj.com/, is billed as "advanced solutions for C/C++ programmers" and is highly respected. I believe anyone can learn from studying its pages.

Dr. Dobb's Journal, www.ddj.com/, is one of the oldest and best-established magazines for the professional programmer. Monthly issues cover a wide variety of programming languages.

Send Us Your Favorite Tips

In your quest for learning, have you ever experienced the sublime moment when you figure out a trick that saves time or trouble? Perhaps you realized that you were taking ten steps to accomplish something that could have taken two. Or you found a little-known workaround that gets great results. If you've discovered a useful tip that helped you program more effectively and you'd like to share it, we'd love to hear from you. Go to our Web site at www.cliffsnotes.com and click the Talk to Us button. If we select your tip, we may publish it as part of CliffsNotes Daily, our exciting, free e-mail newsletter. To find out more or to subscribe to a newsletter, go to www.cliffsnotes.com on the Web.

INDEX

CliffsNotes™

Your shortcut to
success™
for over 40 years

Computers and Software
Confused by computers? Struggling with software? Let
CliffsNotes get you up to speed on the fundamentals —
quickly and easily. Titles include:

> Balancing Your Checkbook with Quicken®
> Buying Your First PC
> Creating a Dynamite PowerPoint® 2000 Presentation
> Making Windows® 98 Work for You
> Setting up a Windows® 98 Home Network
> Upgrading and Repairing Your PC
> Using Your First PC
> Using Your First iMac™
> Writing Your First Computer Program

The Internet
Intrigued by the Internet? Puzzled about life online?
Let *CliffsNotes* show you how to get started with e-mail,
Web surfing, and more. Titles include:

> Buying and Selling on eBay®
> Creating Web Pages with HTML
> Creating Your First Web Page
> Exploring the Internet with Yahoo!®
> Finding a Job on the Web
> Getting on the Internet
> Going Online with AOL®
> Shopping Online Safely

Plants with Seeds

Milkweed

by Dorothy Wood

ILLUSTRATED BY KENYON SHANNON

Follett Publishing Company

Chicago

A sequoia tree

Plants with seeds grow all over the world. They grow in many different sizes and shapes. Some of them are very small; some are very large.

A great sequoia tree is a plant with seeds. These trees are the largest plants we have. They grow in California.

Sequoia trees grow for hundreds of years, getting bigger all the time. Each tree makes seeds, from which new sequoia trees can grow.

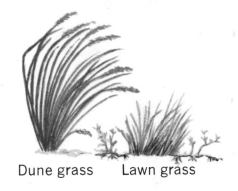

Dune grass   Lawn grass

Grass is a plant.
Each separate plant has
thin leaves called blades.
Each plant has a thin,
tough stem, and tough,
threadlike roots that
spread through the soil.

Prairie grass

There are a great
many different kinds of
grass. These different
kinds grow in a lawn,
in a meadow, in a prairie,
in a desert, or in sand
dunes.

All kinds of grasses
are plants, and each kind
of grass makes seeds.

Meadow grass   Desert grass

5

All our garden flowers and vegetables are
plants, and all these plants make seeds. So
do the bushes and trees around your home,
the trees in the forests, the crops in the fields,
and the weeds and wildflowers by the road.

Water lilies are seed plants. So are the
tiny duckweeds, floating on top of the water.
Duckweeds are the smallest seed plants.

Some kinds of plants do not make seeds. The ferns in the woods are a kind of plant that does not make seeds.

Mosses and mushrooms are plants, and so is the mold that comes on bread, and so is the green scum on a pond or in a bird bath. None of these kinds of plants make seeds.

But the plants we see most often are plants with seeds.

Pond scum

Duckweeds   Water lilies

Plants are alive.
They are alive just as
animals are alive.
Animals grow, and so
do plants. Plants must
have food to live, just
as animals must have
food.

Plants are "living
things." All the living
things in the world are
either plants or animals.

Most kinds of animals
can move around. Plants
must stay in one place.
But plants can make their
own food. Animals cannot.

All plants that make seeds have roots, stems, and leaves.

The roots are the part of the plant that grows down into the ground. They help hold the plant in place.

A big tree has roots that go deep into the ground. The roots spread out in all directions. Above the ground the tree has a big trunk, or stem, that has many branches and leaves.

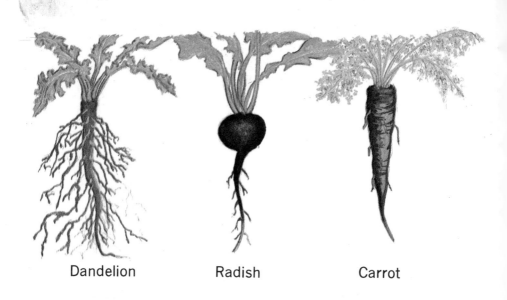

Dandelion   Radish   Carrot

Small plants have roots that do not go down as deep or spread out as much. They have smaller stems and fewer leaves than trees.

Some plants have a big, thick root growing straight down, with smaller roots branching out from it. This large root is called a taproot. A dandelion has a taproot.

Some plants store food in their taproots, and so the taproot becomes thick. Carrots, beets, and radishes are roots that have food stored in them.

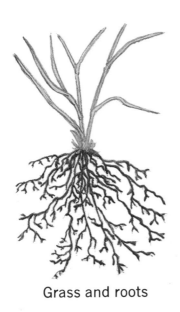

Grass and roots

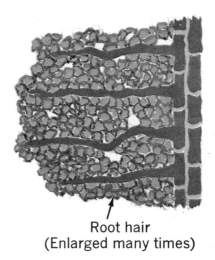

Root hair
(Enlarged many times)

Some plants have many fine roots that branch and spread out in all directions. Grass plants have roots like these.

Roots grow only at their tips or ends. Near the end of each root are tiny branches called root hairs.

Water and minerals from the ground go into these root hairs. The water and minerals travel through the roots, up the stem, and into the leaves.

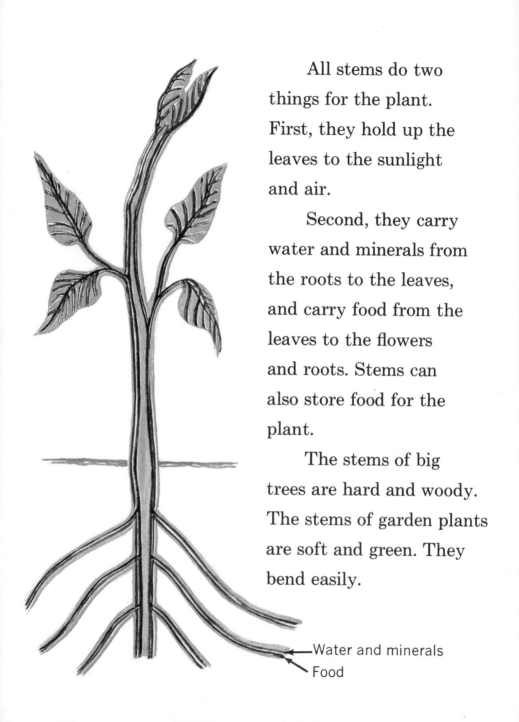

All stems do two things for the plant. First, they hold up the leaves to the sunlight and air.

Second, they carry water and minerals from the roots to the leaves, and carry food from the leaves to the flowers and roots. Stems can also store food for the plant.

The stems of big trees are hard and woody. The stems of garden plants are soft and green. They bend easily.

Water and minerals
Food

Some plants have stems that climb. They are not stiff enough to hold the plant up. They climb on another plant, or on a trellis. Up, up, they go, into the sunlight. The leaves grow from them and spread into the sunlight. Morning glories are vines, and have stems that climb.

Strawberry stems, or runners, grow flat on the ground. They grow out from the plant. Their tips touch the ground, and new plants grow from near the tips. They send roots into the soil, and send up new leaves.

Water lily stems lift leaves and flowers to the top of the water. The stems have air in them; they float upright in the water.

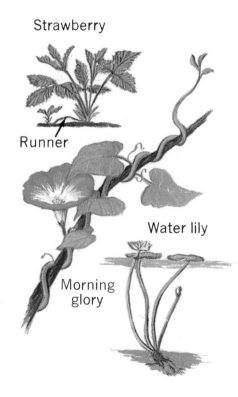

Strawberry

Runner

Water lily

Morning glory

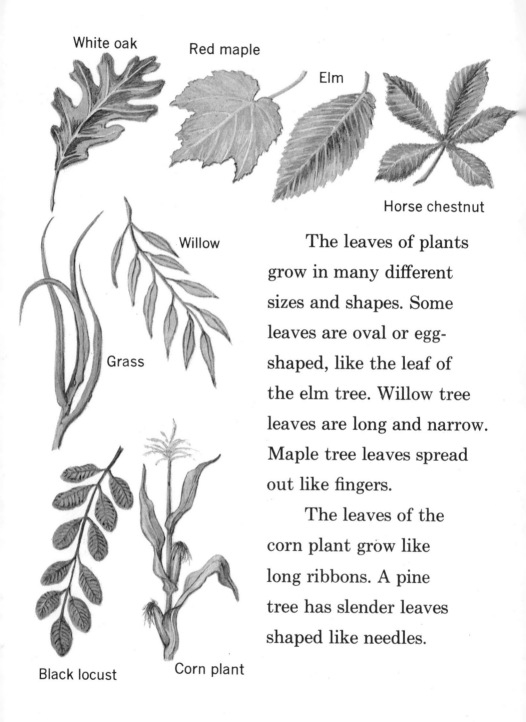

White oak

Red maple

Elm

Horse chestnut

Willow

Grass

Black locust

Corn plant

The leaves of plants grow in many different sizes and shapes. Some leaves are oval or egg-shaped, like the leaf of the elm tree. Willow tree leaves are long and narrow. Maple tree leaves spread out like fingers.

The leaves of the corn plant grow like long ribbons. A pine tree has slender leaves shaped like needles.

Leaves have different kinds of edges. The willow tree leaf has smooth edges. Oak leaves have deeply-cut edges. Elm leaves have edges like saw teeth.

There are two parts to a leaf. There is a flat part called the blade, and there is a supporting stem called a petiole. In some plants, like the oak tree, each leaf is joined separately to a branch. Others, like the horse chestnut or black locust, have several leaflets joined together to make a single leaf.

Leaves have veins running through them. In the leaves of grass plants, the veins run side by side straight from the bottom of the leaf to the top. In maple and sycamore leaves there are many large veins that branch out to all parts of the plant. In an elm leaf, one large vein runs along the whole leaf, and smaller veins branch off on each side of the large vein.

Leaves are a very important part of plants. They make the food for the plant from air and water.

A plant needs two things to change air and water into food. It needs sunlight, and it needs chlorophyll. Chlorophyll is the green coloring of plants. Without chlorophyll the plant cannot make food.

Photosynthesis is the name for the food making of plants. "Photo" means light. "Synthesis" means to put together. So photosynthesis is the putting together of water and air, using sunlight and chlorophyll, to make food for the plant.

A leaf has tiny openings in it, called stomata. "Stomata" means "little mouths."

A gas in the air, called carbon dioxide, goes into the stomata. At the same time water comes up from the roots and stem into the leaves.

Sunlight and chlorophyll help turn carbon dioxide and water into food for the plant. Sugar is made, and most of the sugar soon turns into starch. A gas called oxygen is given off. Animals breathe oxygen.

So, for a plant to make food, it must have four things: carbon dioxide, water, sunlight, and chlorophyll.

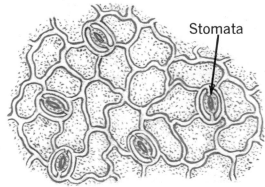

Stomata

17

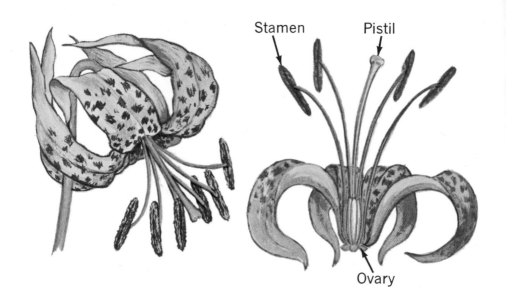

Stamen Pistil

Ovary

Most of the plants around us have flowers.
Many flowers have bright colors and smell sweet.
They make our homes and gardens beautiful. But
that is not all they do.

Flowers make seeds. Seeds grow from the
flowers. They grow as the flower dries up and
dies. We say the flower has "gone to seed."

The picture shows the parts of a flower
that make seeds. In the center of the flower
is the pistil. At the bottom of the pistil is
the ovary, where tiny eggs grow.

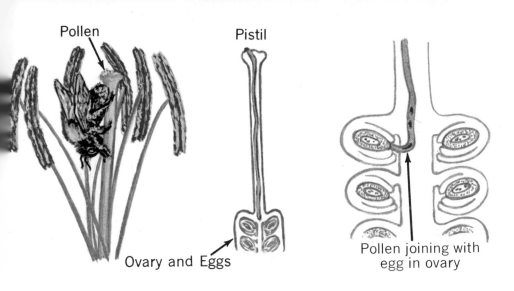

Pollen

Pistil

Ovary and Eggs

Pollen joining with egg in ovary

Around the pistil are long slender parts called stamens. At the tips of the stamens grows a fine powder called pollen.

Pollen falls off the stamens when the wind blows or when a bee visits the flowers.

The tip of the pistil is sticky. When pollen falls on this tip, some pollen sticks to it. From each bit of pollen a tiny tube grows down to the bottom of the pistil.

The pollen travels down each tiny tube and joins with an egg in the ovary. Then seeds can grow from the egg.

After the pollen joins with an egg, the petals of the flower fall off. The ovary gets bigger and becomes a fruit. The fruit holds the seeds inside it and protects the seeds. All flowering plants grow fruits with seeds in them.

Some fruits are soft and juicy and good to eat. We call them fleshy fruits. Apples, pears, and oranges are fleshy fruits.

Some fruits are dry and hard. We call them dry fruits. Beans and peas in their pods and nuts in their shells are dry fruits. Maple and elm trees have dry fruits. So do corn, wheat, poppy, and lily plants.

Apple fruit

Apple fruit growing

Some fleshy fruits have two parts. The outside is soft and juicy. The inside is hard and stony, with one or two seeds in it. We eat the outside part and throw the inside part away. Peaches, plums, apricots, and cherries are fruits of this kind.

Raspberries and blackberries are really many fruits that are joined together. Each little round part is a tiny fruit with one seed in it.

Some fruits have just one seed in them, like the acorn. Other fruits have many seeds, like the watermelon or the pumpkin.

Peach seed

Apple seeds

Ripe apple fruit

Strawberry

Raspberry

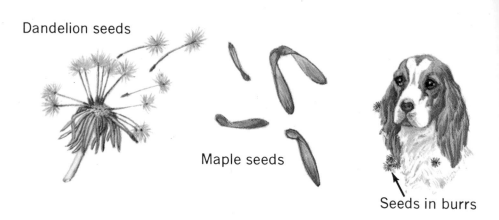

Dandelion seeds

Maple seeds

Seeds in burrs

When the fruit is ripe, the seeds are ready to grow into new plants. The plant then drops its seeds to the ground.

The seeds travel to the ground in many ways. Some seeds, like maple seeds, have wings. They spin around and around as they fall down.

Some seeds, like peas and beans, are in pods. The pods open, and the seeds fall to the ground. Other seeds, like the dandelion seeds, have tiny parachutes and float away.

The seeds of some plants are inside burrs that have sharp hooks. The hooks stick to clothes or fur, and the burrs are pulled off and carried away.

All seeds have three things. They have a seed coat around them. They have a tiny plant inside them. And they have food in them for the plant while it is growing.

In the ground the seed takes in water. The seed swells up and breaks open the seed coat. The plant begins to grow. A tiny root grows down. A tiny stem with leaves grows up.

The new plant uses the food from the seed until it has grown big enough to make its food.

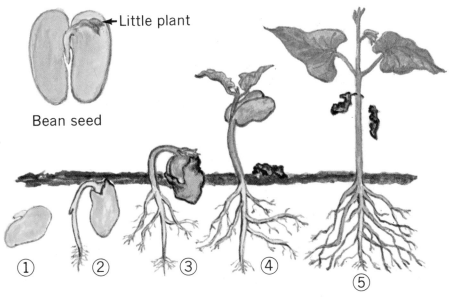

←Little plant

Bean seed

① ② ③ ④ ⑤

Follow the numbers from 1 to 5 to see how a bean plant grows from a seed

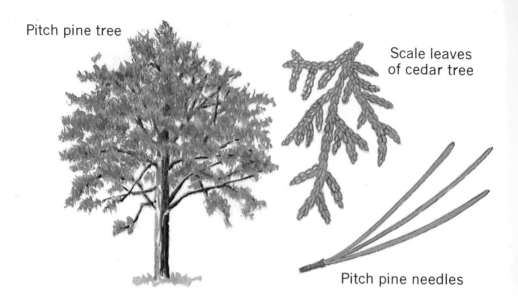

Pitch pine tree

Scale leaves
of cedar tree

Pitch pine needles

Some plants, such as the pine tree, do not ever have flowers. They have cones instead. Their seeds grow in the cones.

The fir, the spruce, and the hemlock trees all have cones. We call these tree conifers.

Some of the conifers have needles. Others have tiny leaves like the scales of a fish.

Most conifers keep their leaves all year. The leaves stay green all winter. This is why conifers are often called evergreen trees.

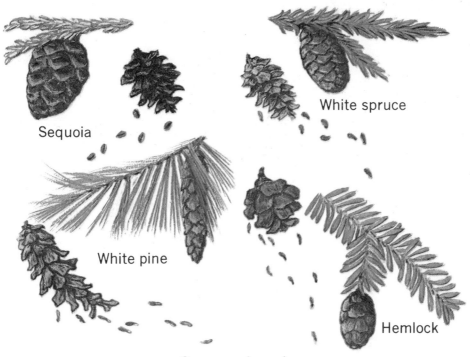

Sequoia

White spruce

White pine

Hemlock

Cones and seeds

The seeds and the cone grow along together. In some kinds of conifers they grow for several years. When the seeds are ready, the cone spreads open, and the seeds fall to the ground.

Some conifer seeds have wings and are carried along by the wind. Some of them have sharp points and plant themselves in the ground as they fall.

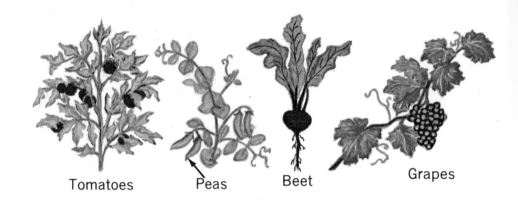

Tomatoes   Peas   Beet   Grapes

If plants did not make food, there would
be no food for the living things on the earth.
Air, water, and sunlight are not food. But
plants can use these things to make food.

People cannot make food from air and water
and sunlight. Plants are the only living things
that can do this. They make food for all the
living things on the earth.

They make all the vegetables that we eat
—the beans, peas and corn, the lettuce, tomatoes,
and carrots, and all the others. They make our
fruits, too—apples and oranges and all kinds
of berries.

Flour for bread and cakes is made from
the wheat plant. Cereals are made from wheat,
corn, and rice plants.

Grass, hay, and corn are food for the cows
that give us milk and butter. Beef cattle and
the pigs and sheep that give us meat also
eat these foods.

Like other living creatures, people depend
upon plants for all their food.

Plants help us in many other ways.

All our wood comes from plants. Pine trees and oak trees give us lumber to build houses and stores and bridges. From maple and walnut trees comes the wood for much of our furniture.

Paper comes from plants, too. It is made from the trunks of trees. So without plants, we would have nothing made of paper—no writing paper, or wrapping paper, or pasteboard boxes, or paper plates or cups for picnics. There would be no books or newspapers.

Many of the things we wear come from plants. Cotton plants give us material for dresses and shirts and towels and many other things we use around our homes. Linen comes from flax plants. Hemp for rope comes from hemp plants. Rubber is made from the sap of rubber trees.

Turpentine comes from the sap of pine trees, and many medicines are made from plants.

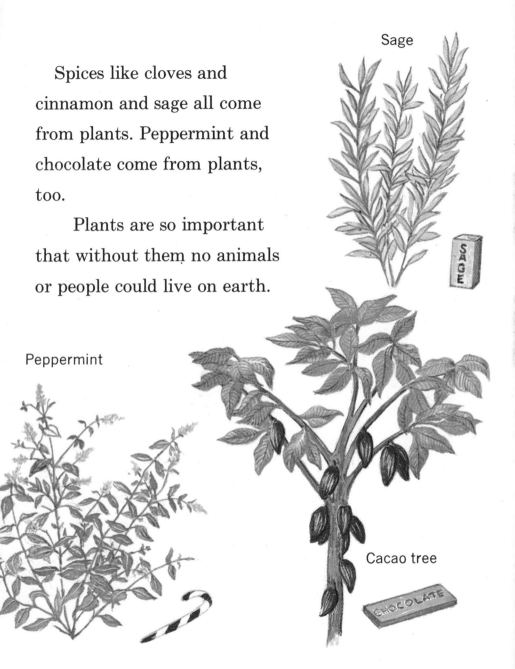

Spices like cloves and cinnamon and sage all come from plants. Peppermint and chocolate come from plants, too.

Plants are so important that without them no animals or people could live on earth.

Sage

Peppermint

Cacao tree

CHOCOLATE

SAGE

Words Younger Children May Need Help With

(Numbers refer to page on which the word first appears.)

4	sequoia		oval	21	apricots
	California	15	edges		raspberries
5	separate		supporting		acorn
	blades		petiole	22	burrs
	tough		leaflets		parachutes
	threadlike		single	24	fir
	lawn		veins		spruce
	meadow	16	chlorophyll		hemlock
	prairie		photosynthesis		conifers
	desert		stomata		scales
	dunes		carbon dioxide		pitch pine
6	duckweeds		oxygen	27	creatures
7	mushrooms	18	pistil	28	walnut
	scum		ovary		pasteboard
10	dandelion		stamen		turpentine
	radish	19	pollen		medicines
11	minerals		tube	29	spices
13	morning glories	20	petals		cloves
	strawberry		protects		cinnamon
14	horse chestnut		juicy		sage
	willow		fleshy		peppermint
	black locust		pods		chocolate

THINGS TO DO IN THE CLASSROOM OR AT HOME

Look at roots and root hairs. Go to an empty grass lot where dandelions are growing. Dig up the earth carefully around the dandelion root. Keep on digging until you can take out the whole dandelion plant, root and all. See how long the dandelion root is. The dandelion root is a taproot. It is a big thick root with a few smaller roots branching out from it. Now dig up a clump of grass the very same way. Grass roots are diffuse roots.

Diffuse roots are many small roots that branch and spread out in all directions.

Dig up a tall weed that has leaves on it. What kind of root does it have? See the fine root hairs branch off the end of the roots.

See how stems carry water to the leaves. Get a stalk of celery. Put some red food coloring into a glass of water. You can get red food coloring at the market. Put in enough coloring to make the water dark red. Put the celery stalk in the water and let it stand overnight. The next day you will see that the red water has traveled up the stalk. Cut off a piece of the bottom part of the stalk. You will see the hollow tubes filled with red water.

Put a white carnation in the red water. The next day the petals of the carnation will have red in them, because the water traveled up the stem and into the petals. If you can find a white carnation with a thick stem, split the bottom part of the stem into two parts with a scissors. Fill two glasses with colored water, one red and one blue, and put the glasses side by side. Put one part of the split stem in the glass of red water, and the other part in the glass of blue water. The next day the petals of the carnation will be a pretty red, white, and blue.

Collect and identify different kinds of leaves. See how they have different sizes and shapes. Note the different edges on the leaves. Look at the veins on the leaves and see how they are arranged.

Show that leaves make food for the plant. Pull off a geranium leaf that has been in the sun for many hours. Ask your mother to set up a double boiler. Put water in the bottom part of the boiler, and some rubbing alcohol in the top part of the boiler. Put the geranium leaf in the alcohol in the top part of the boiler. Now heat the double boiler on the stove. The alcohol will turn green. The green coloring is chlorophyll that has come out of the leaf. After a few minutes take the boiler off the stove. Pour the chlorophyll and alcohol into the sink and put the geranium leaf on a plate. The leaf will be pale now, because it has lost its chlorophyll. Get a bottle of iodine used for putting on cuts. Get a potato, too. Cut the potato in half. Put a drop or two of iodine on the white part of the potato. The strawberry color of the iodine will turn a deep purple. A potato has lots of starch in it. A test for starch is to add iodine. If the iodine turns deep purple, there is starch. Now put a drop or two of iodine on your geranium leaf. The iodine will turn deep purple, showing that the leaf has starch in it.

Examine a flower. Get a large simple flower like a tulip or a lily. Find the pistil. See the stamens that are around the pistil. How many stamens are there? Is there any pollen on the tips of the stamens?

See how a plant grows from a seed. Get a lima bean and put it in a glass of water overnight. The lima bean is a seed of the lima bean plant. In the morning take the bean out of the water. See how the bean has swelled because water has got into it. First, peel off the colorless seed coat. Now, with your fingernails split open the two halves of the bean. Inside one of these halves you will see a tiny plant. When the tiny plant begins to grow, it will take its food from the halves of the seed until the new plant can make its own food.

Look at all the fruits in a supermarket. Which fruits are fleshy? Which ones are dry? Which fruits have one seed? Many seeds? Which fruits have a fleshy part and a hard inside part with one or two seeds in it? Which fruits are made up of many fruits that are all joined together? What kind of coverings do the fruits have?